NICOLAS VALLET

Le Secret des Muses

Transcribed for Classical Guitar

PAUL MASCOTT

WWW.MELBAY.COM

Preface

The lute music of Nicolas Vallet (c.1583 – c.1642) represents a musical bridge between Renaissance and Baroque sensibilities in Europe and as a body of work provides entertaining material in transcription for beginning to advanced classical guitar players. At times his music seems fully Baroque in character containing running lines of sequences and counterpoint while at other moments the works give a solid sense of the traditional lute techniques of the day. His music is mostly tonal with hints at older modal approaches, and sometimes contains surprising and interesting modulations especially in his Fantasies.

Most of what is known about Vallet comes from his music and a selection of contracts and legal papers contained in the city archives of Amsterdam. He was born in France around 1583 and relocated to Amsterdam by 1614 where he worked as a lute teacher, headed a band that played weddings and festivals, and was also the owner of a dance school. He was held in high regard and published several collections of lute music in the years following his move, including vocal settings of psalms and church music.

Le Secret des Muses is among the last published collections of lute music intended for the Renaissance 10-course lute before the instrument was supplanted by the larger 13-course lute throughout Europe in the coming decades. The manuscript is written in French lute tablature and broken into two volumes with 132 pieces total (including nine lute quartets). Of note in the original edition is the attention paid to the right-hand fingerings which has provided a useful window into the interpretation of other works from the period as well. Most of the pieces are traditional dance forms from around Europe along with several interesting fantasies and a number of settings of traditional lute themes. The volumes were published in Amsterdam in 1615 and 1616 and then released again in France in 1618 and 1619. The transcription in this edition was taken from the later publications.

This book contains 53 of the easier pieces from the full collection including a handful of longer works appropriate for concert applications. In addition, the piece "Babdaille" is a useful warm-up piece for students.

There are specifically two ornaments used throughout *Le Secret des Muses* – appogiatura and trill. The appogiaturas are written out and are generally executed using simple pull-offs. The trill or "shake" can simply be defined as a rapid alternation between two notes. In this edition it is assumed that the trill note is the next step above the marked note.

Contents

1. L'Espagnolle

Nicolas Vallet

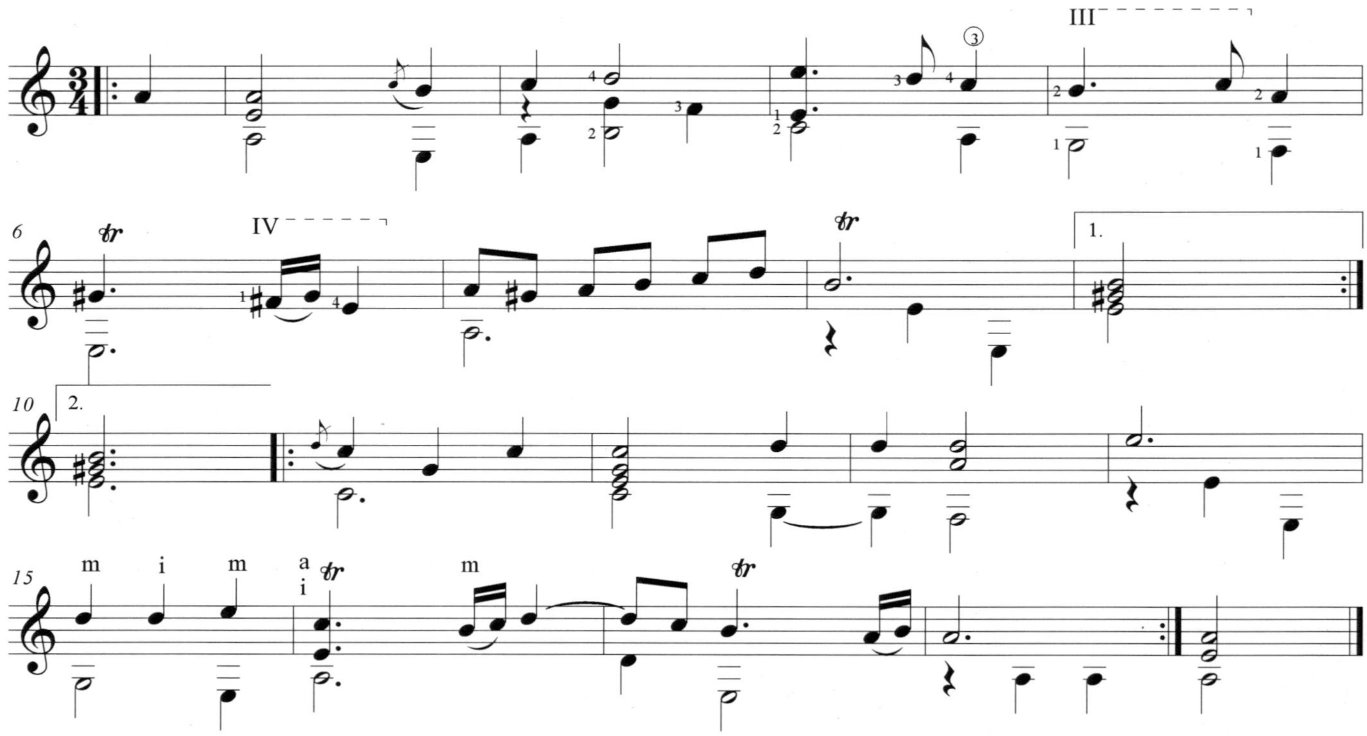

2. Bourée

Nicolas Vallet

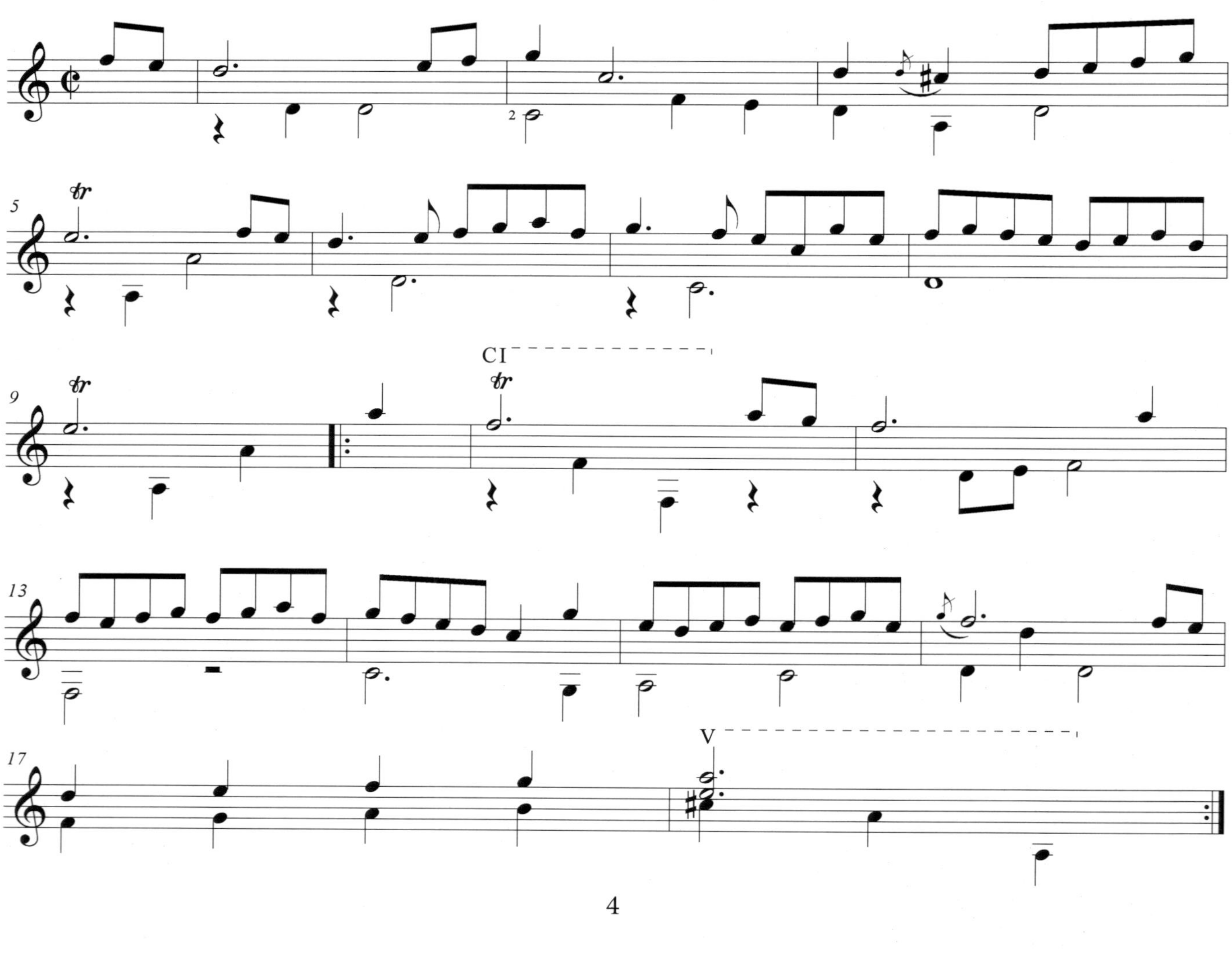

3. La Sarabande Espagnole

Nicolas Vallet

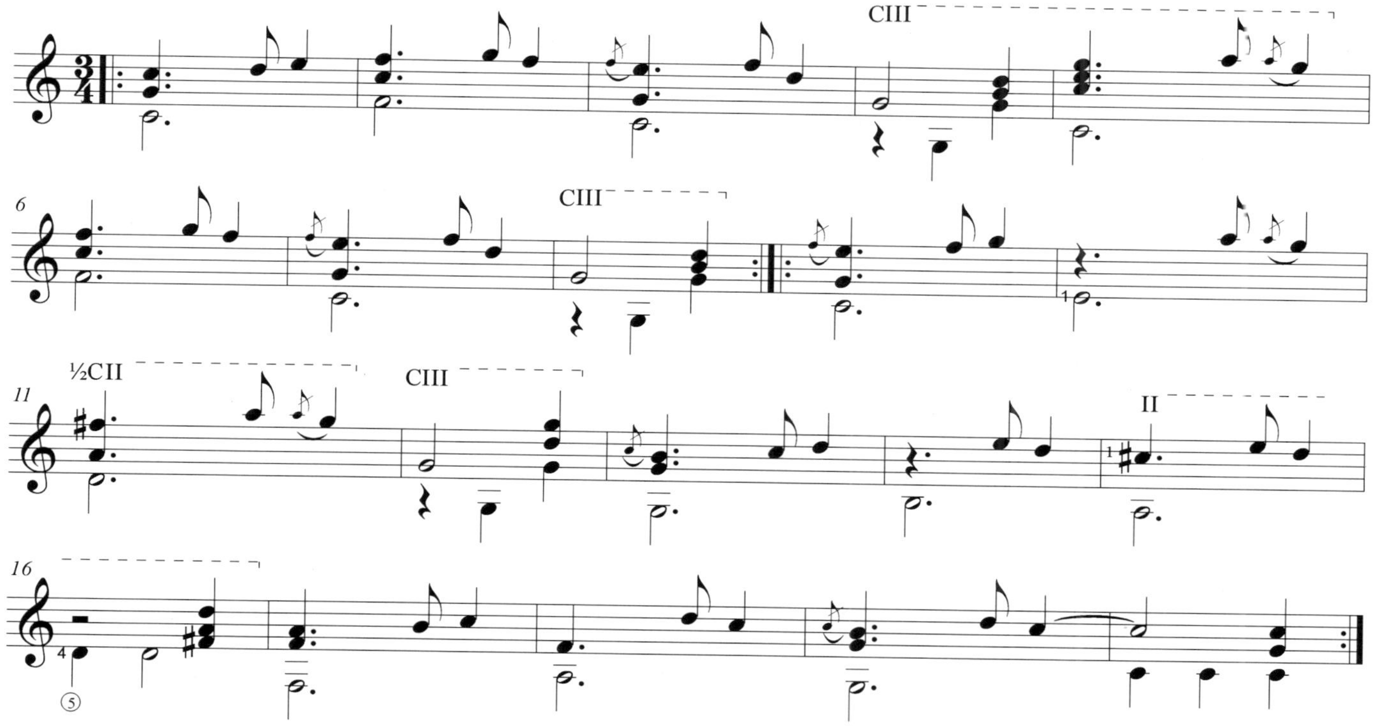

4. Volte du Roi

Nicolas Vallet

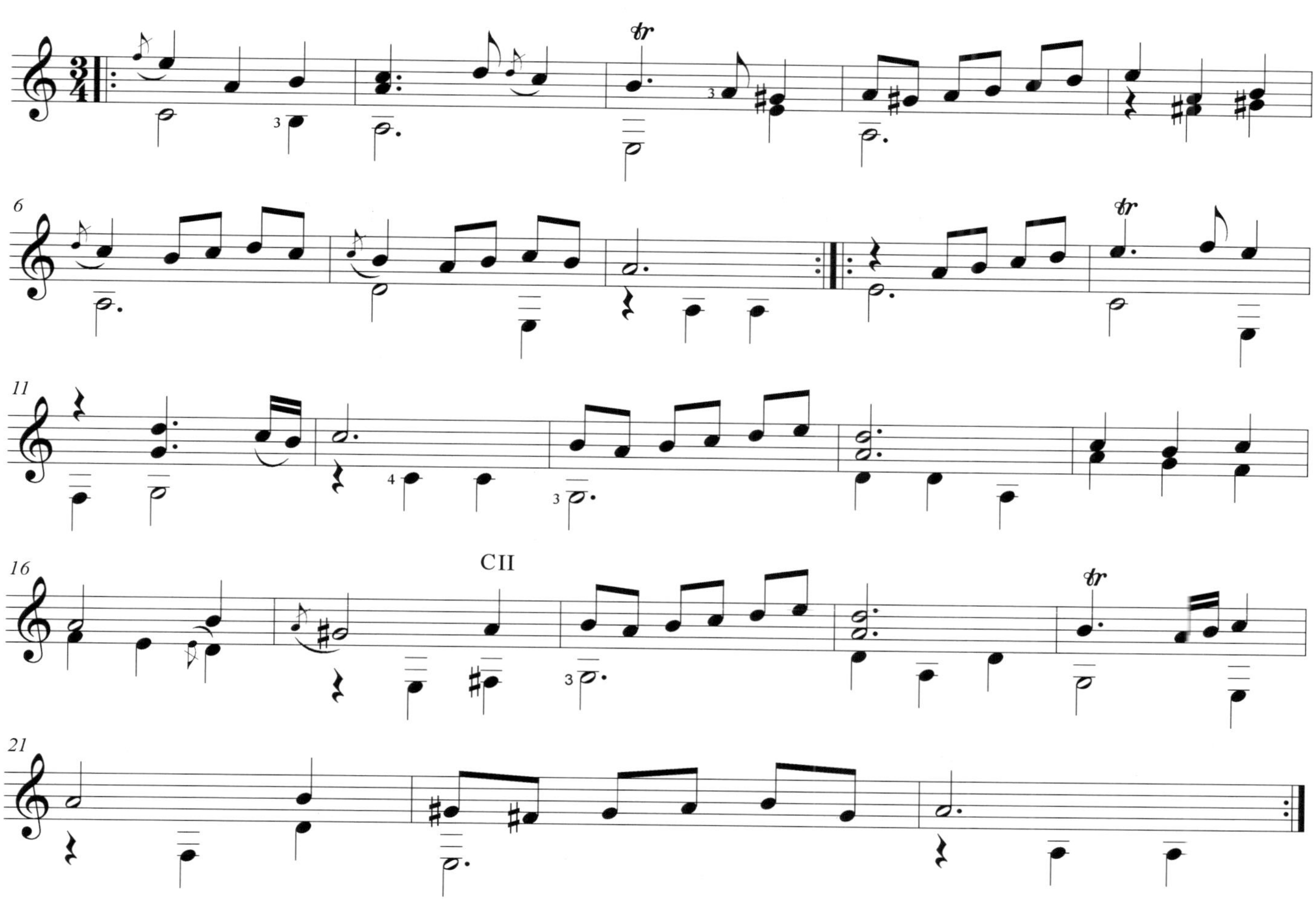

5. Volte

Nicolas Vallet

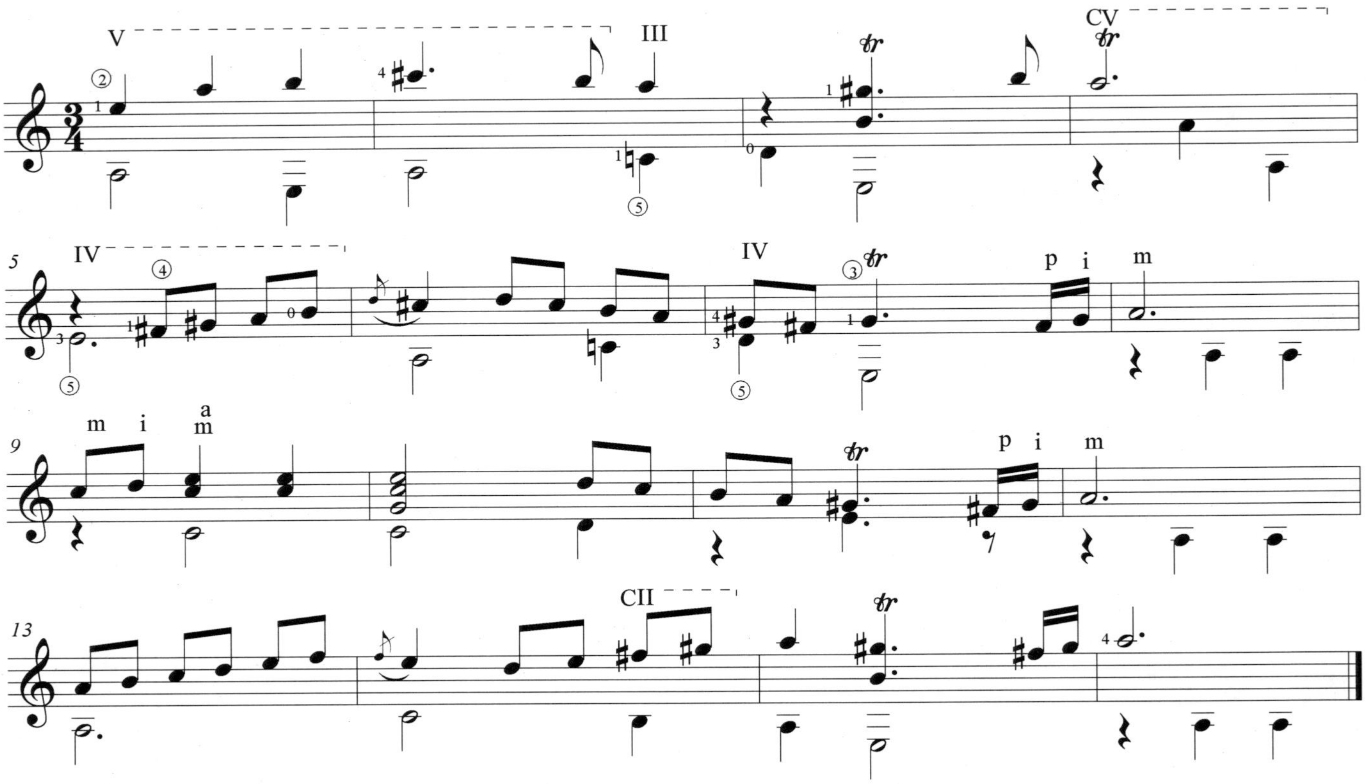

6. Volte

Nicolas Vallet

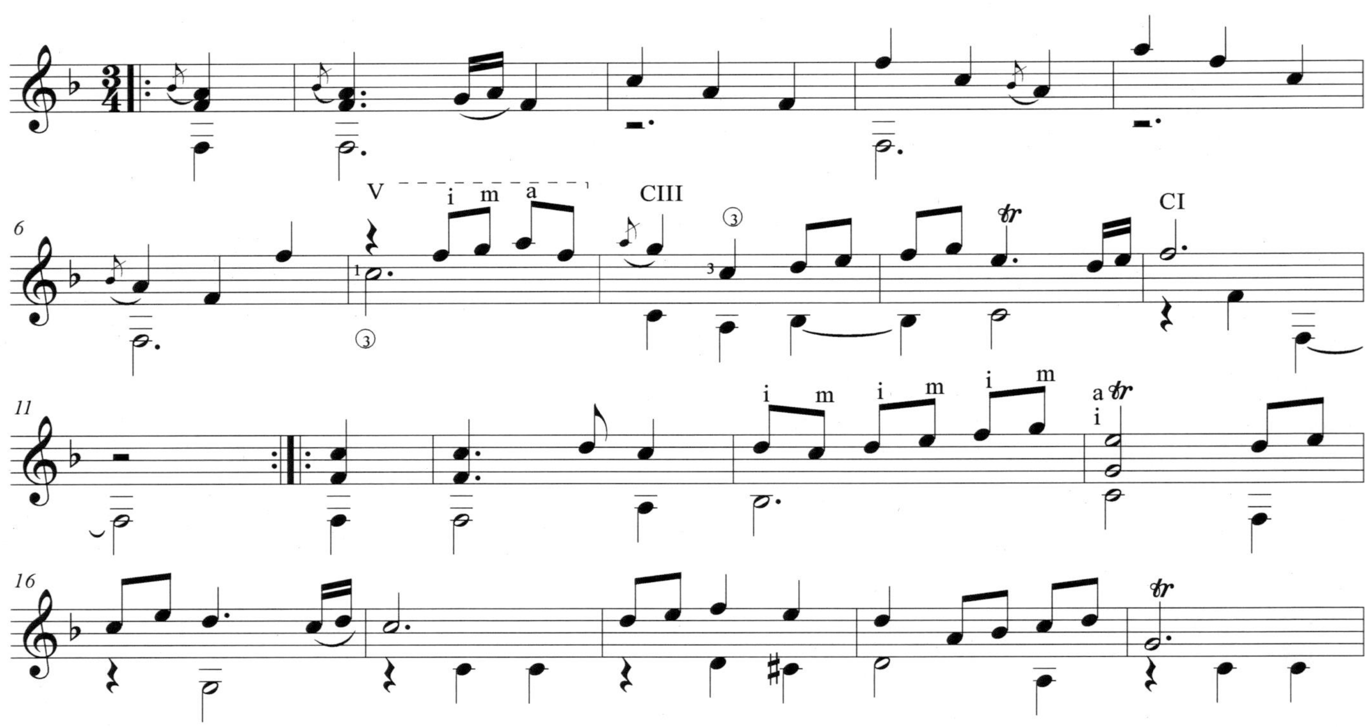

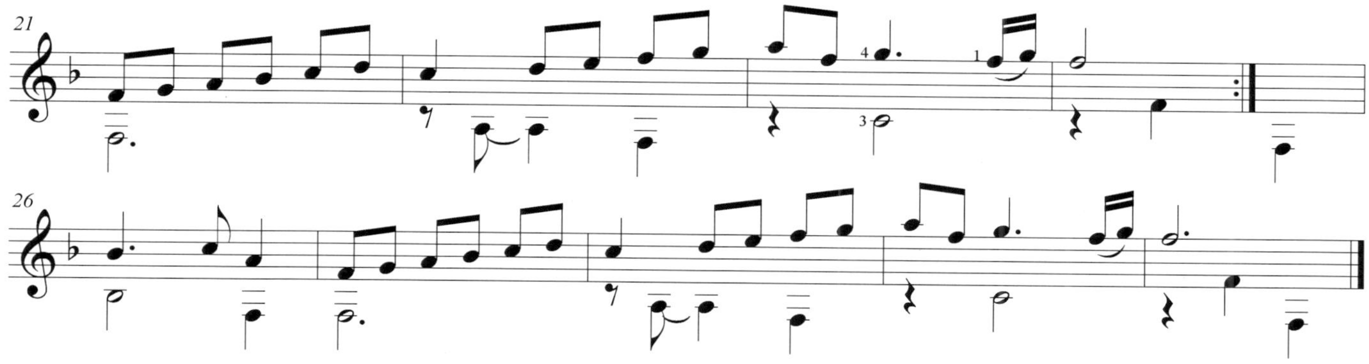

7. La Daulphine

Nicolas Vallet

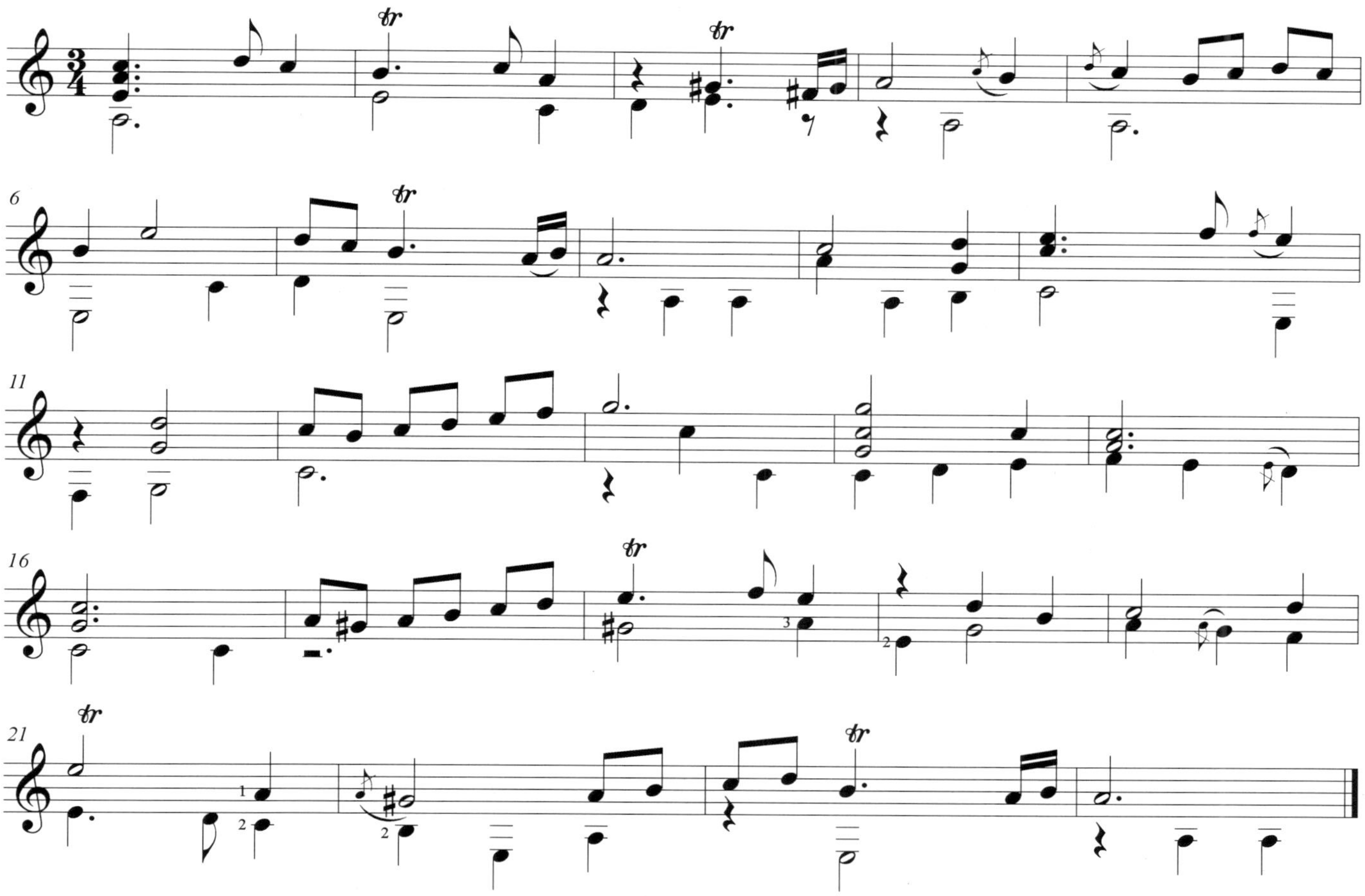

8. Bourée

Nicolas Vallet

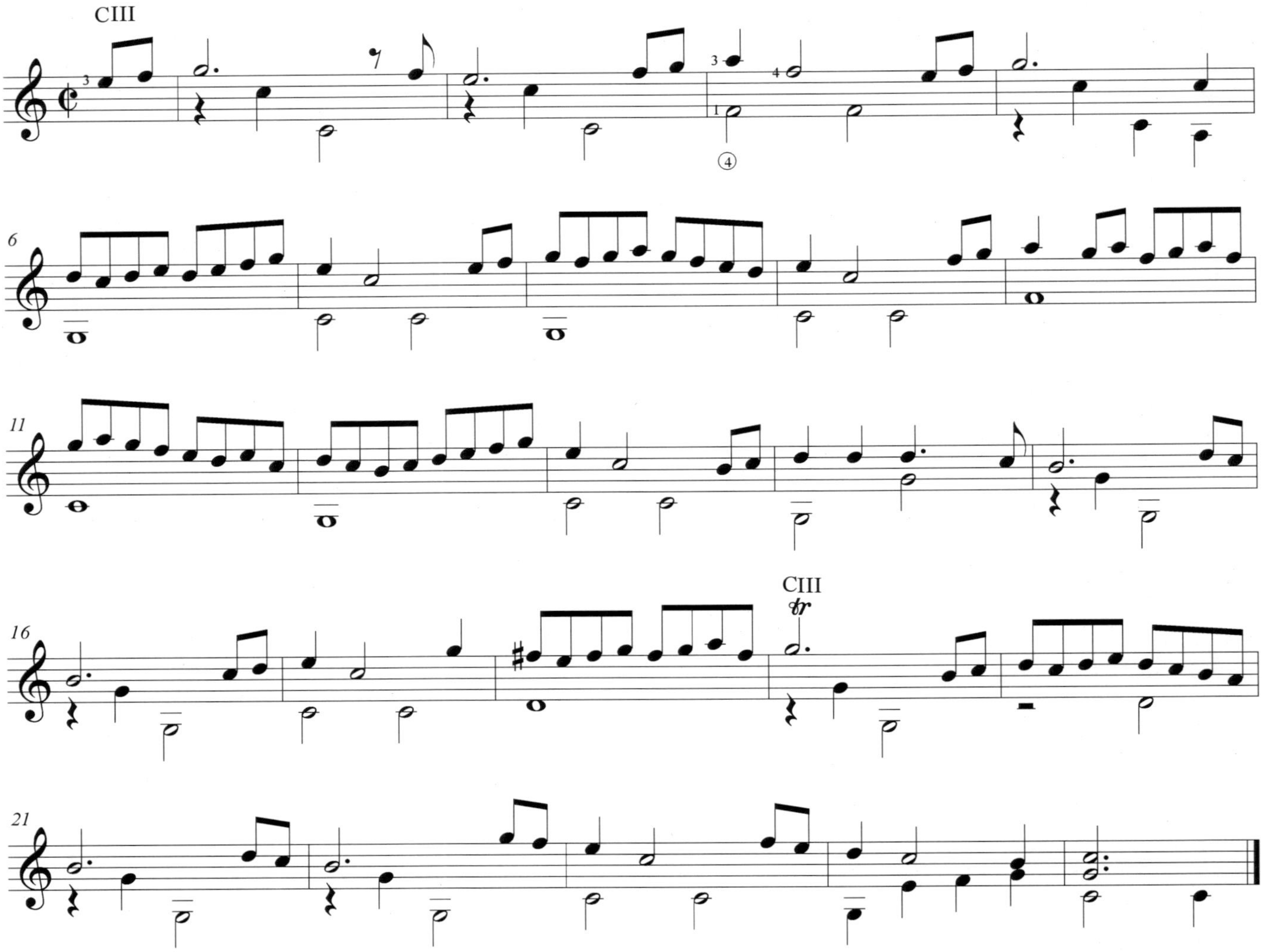

9. Lamoresque

Nicolas Vallet

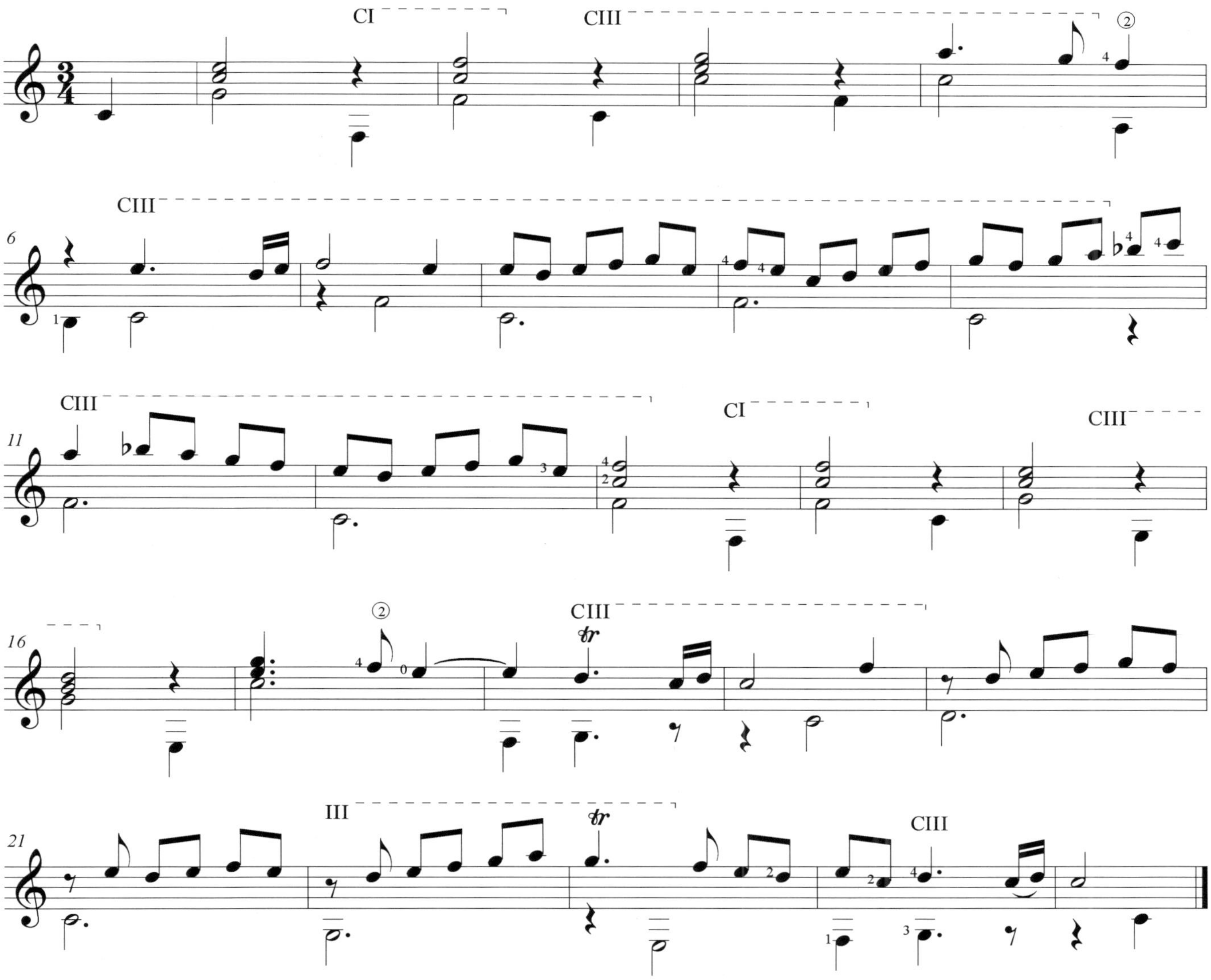

10. Ballet

Nicolas Vallet

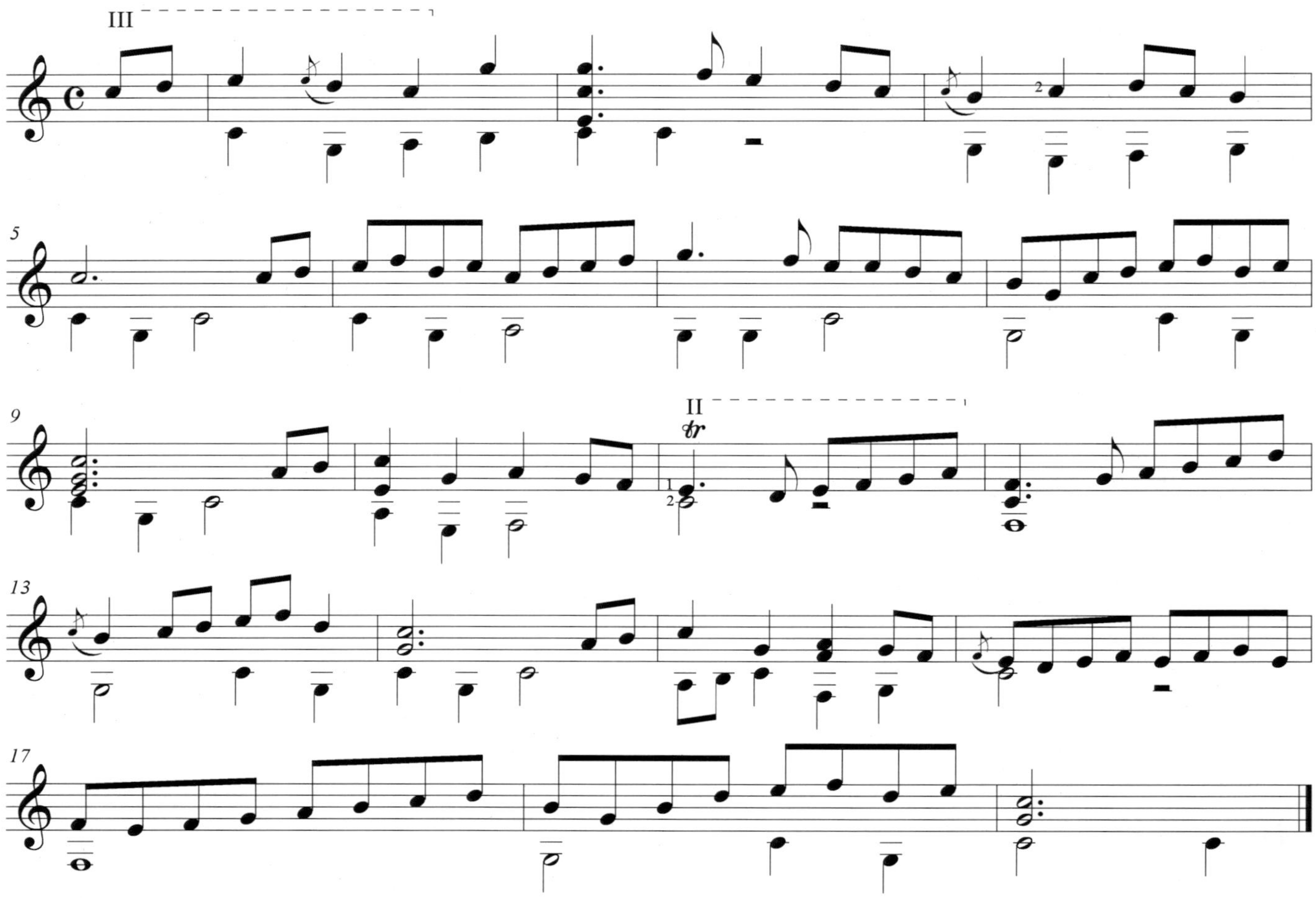

11. Ballet

Nicolas Vallet

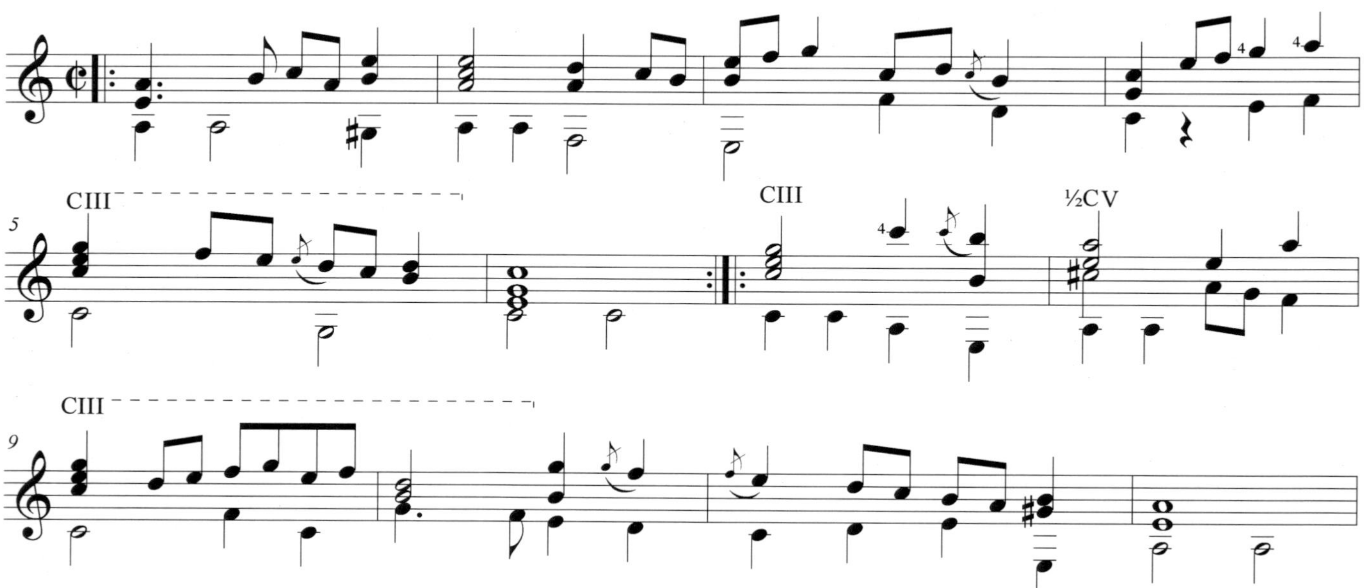

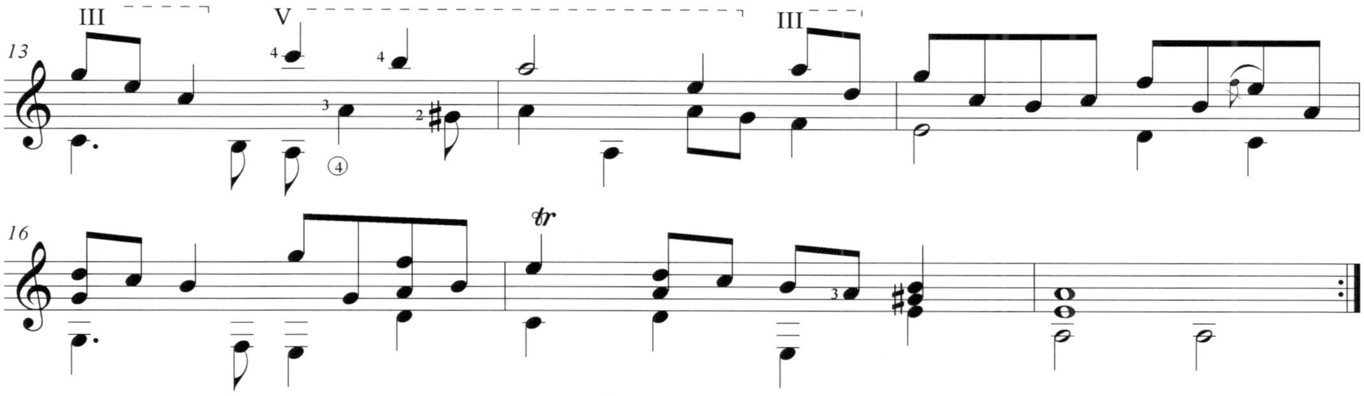

12. Ballet

Nicolas Vallet

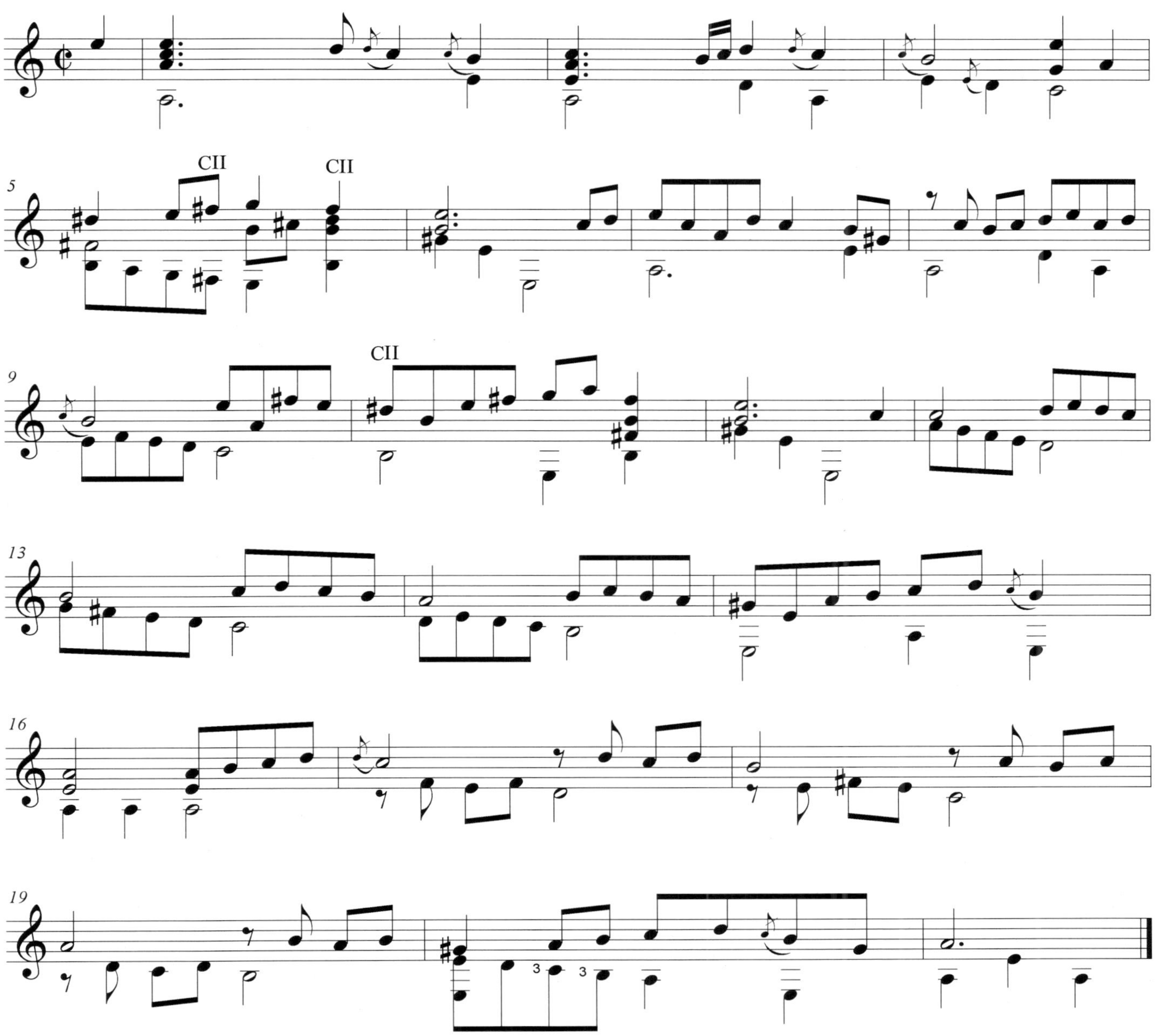

13. La Chacone

Nicolas Vallet

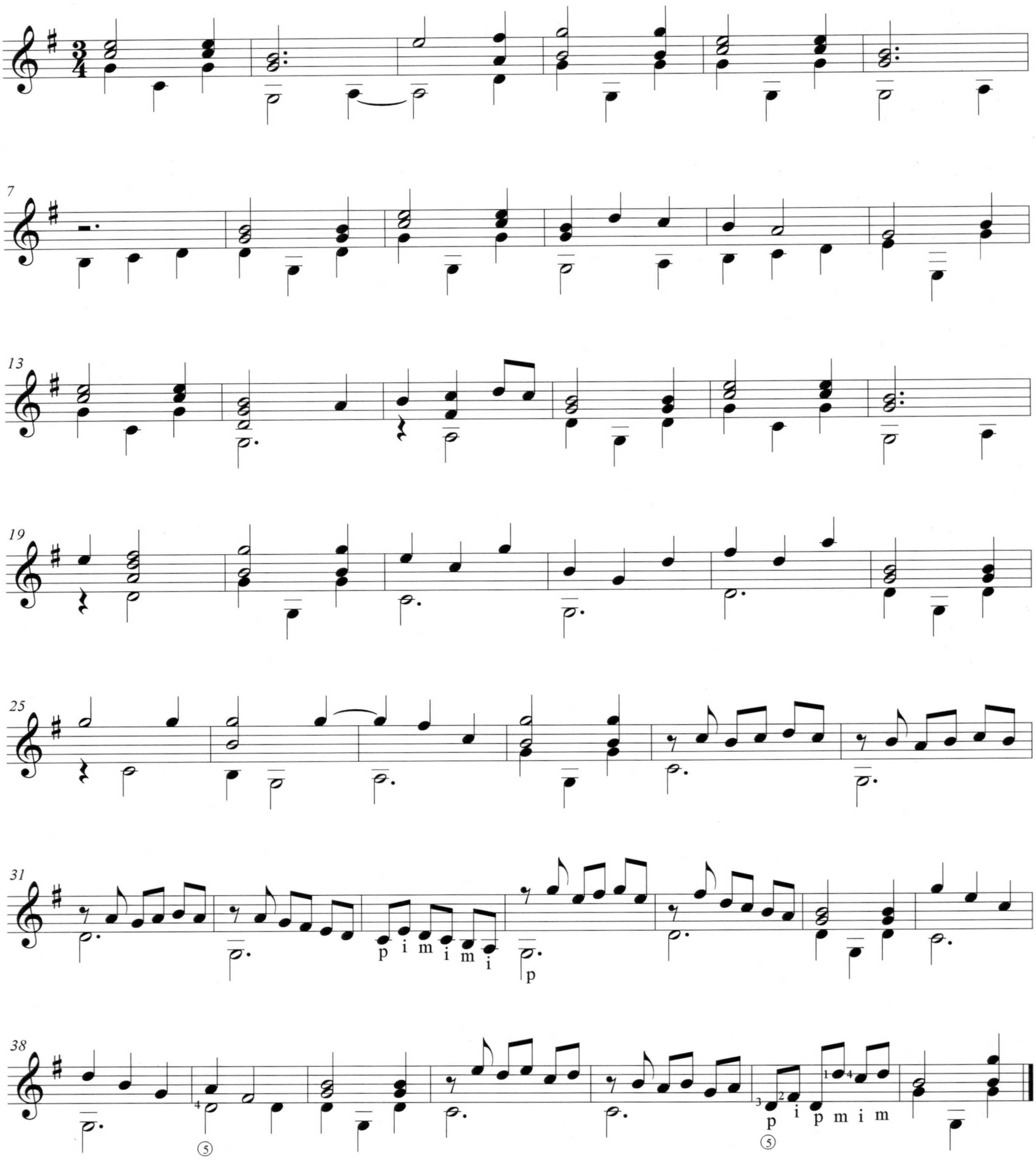

14. Pavanne de Spagne

Nicolas Vallet

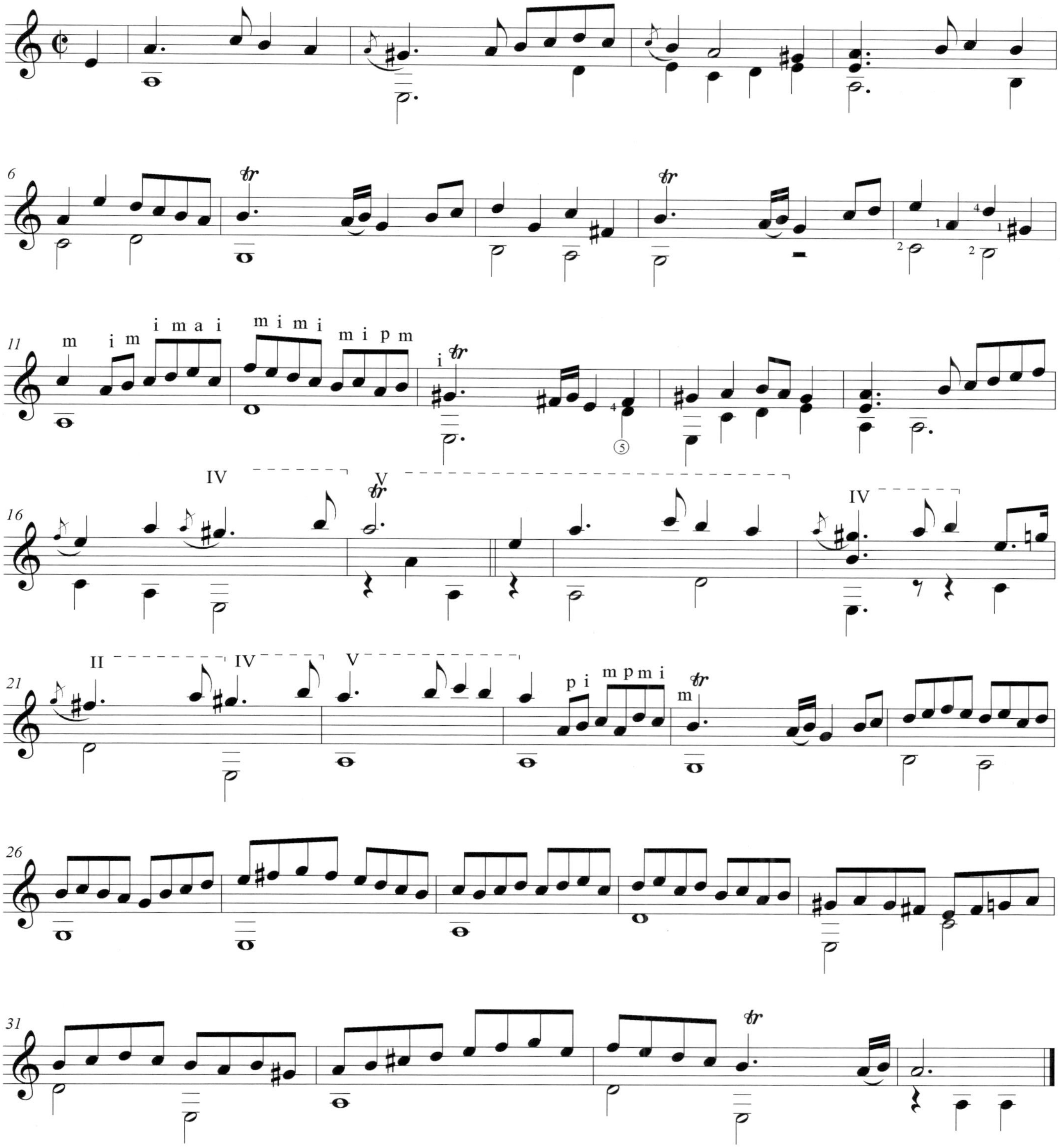

15. Malsimmes

Nicolas Vallet

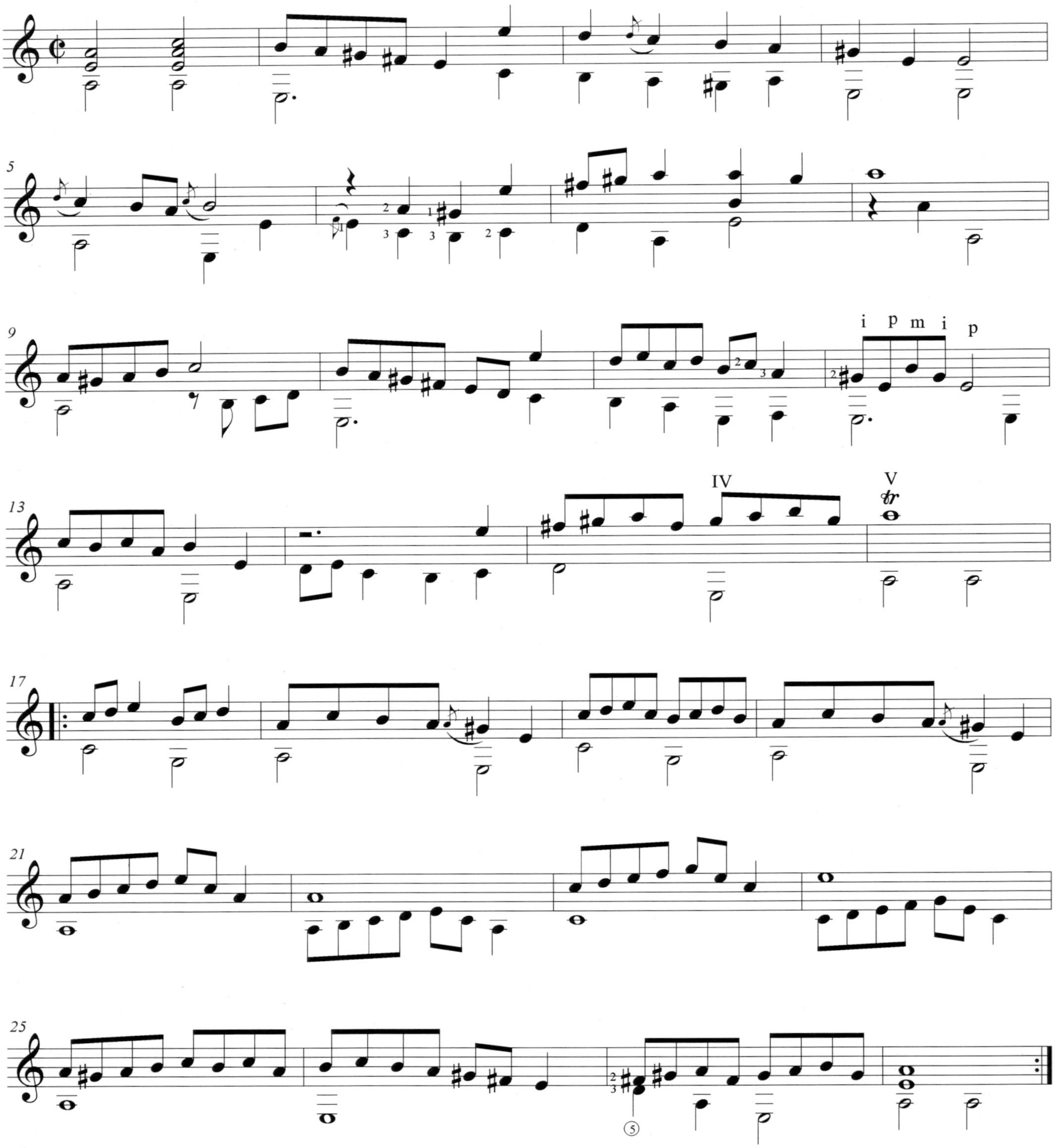

16. L'auignonne

Nicolas Vallet

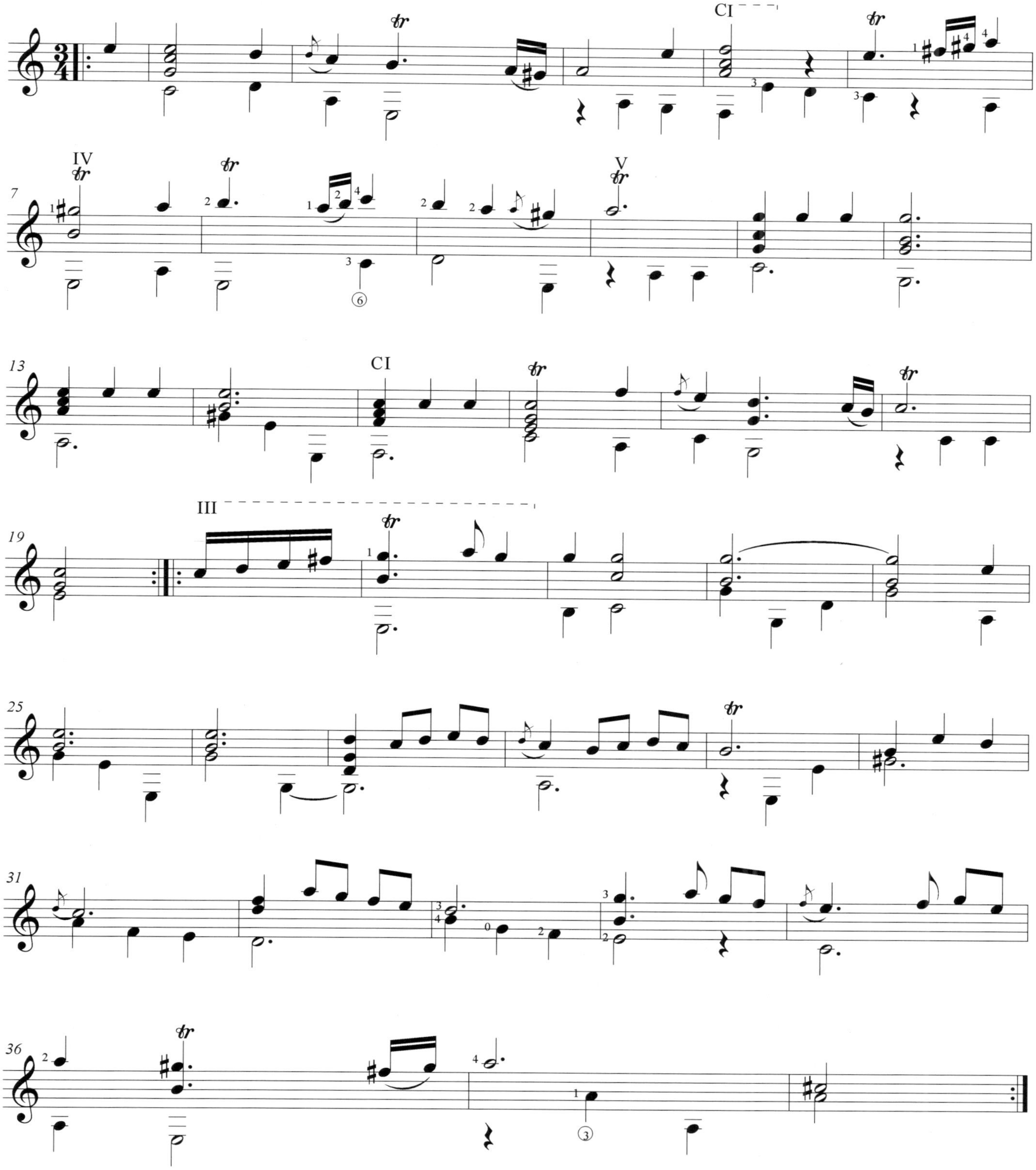

17. La Durette

Nicolas Vallet

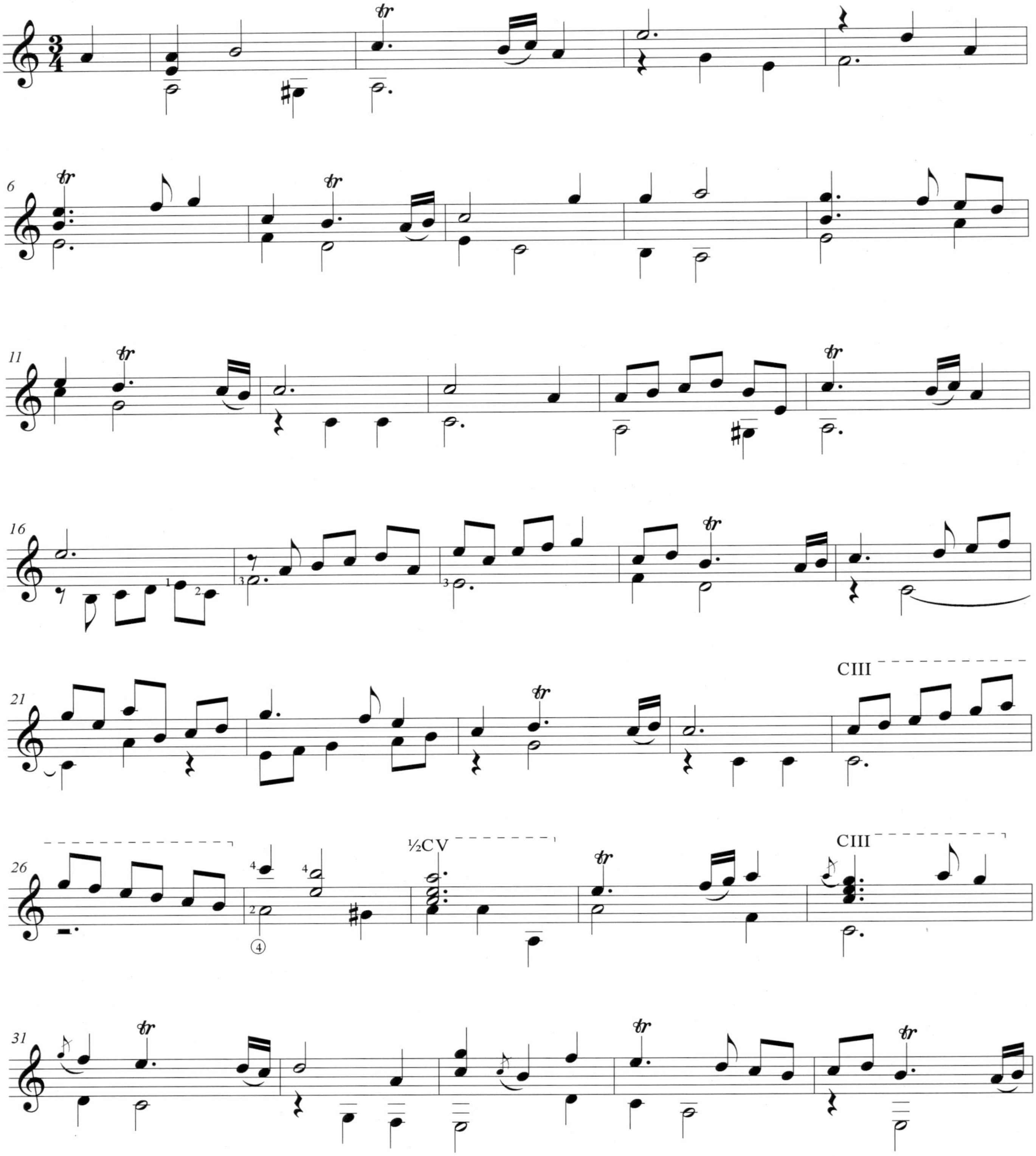

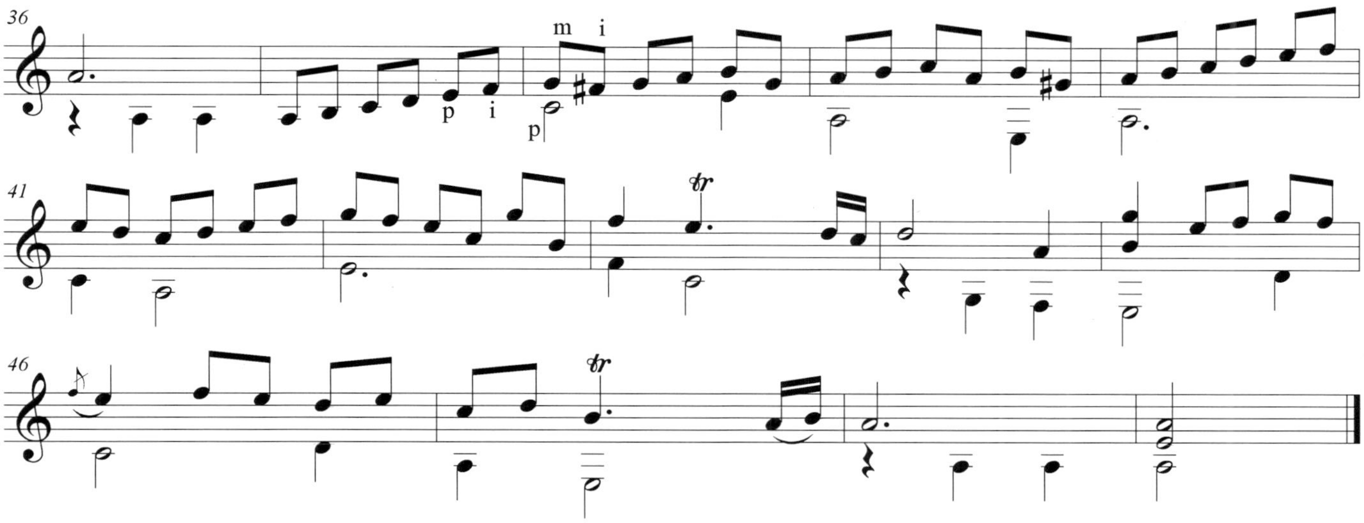
36
m i
p i
p
41
tr
46
tr

18. La Signolle

Nicolas Vallet

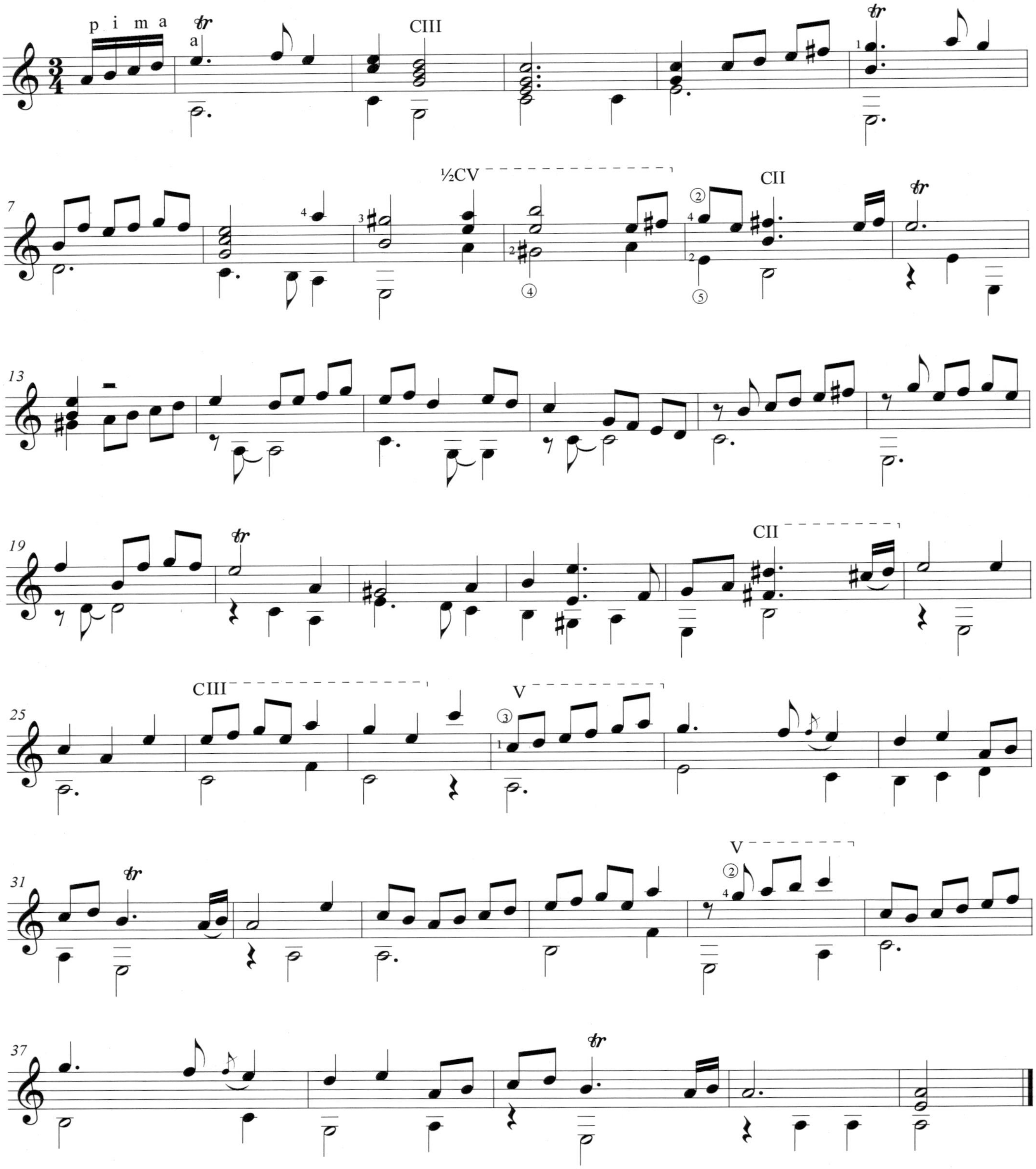

19. Bourée de Village

Nicolas Vallet

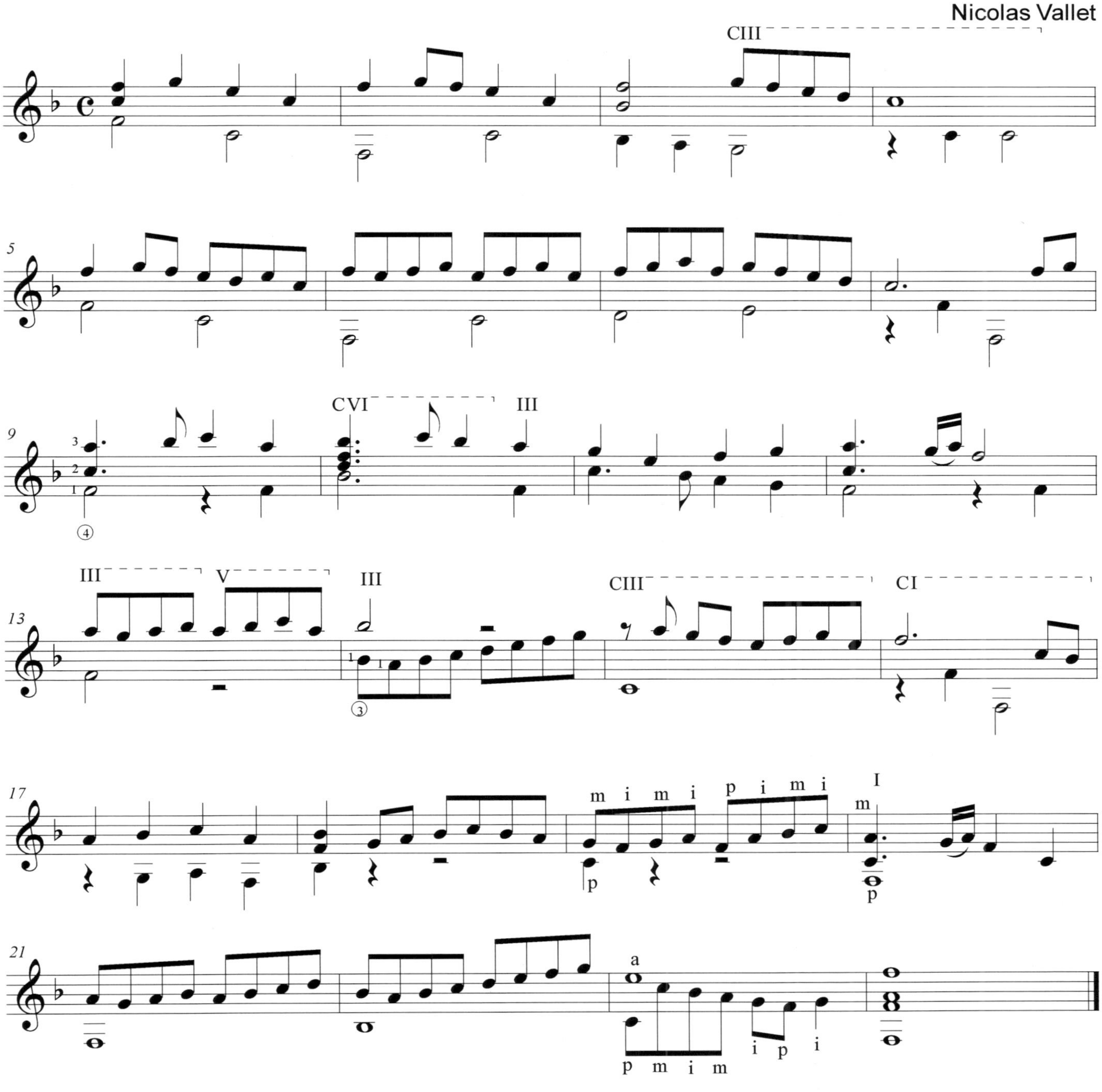

20. Bourée

Nicolas Vallet

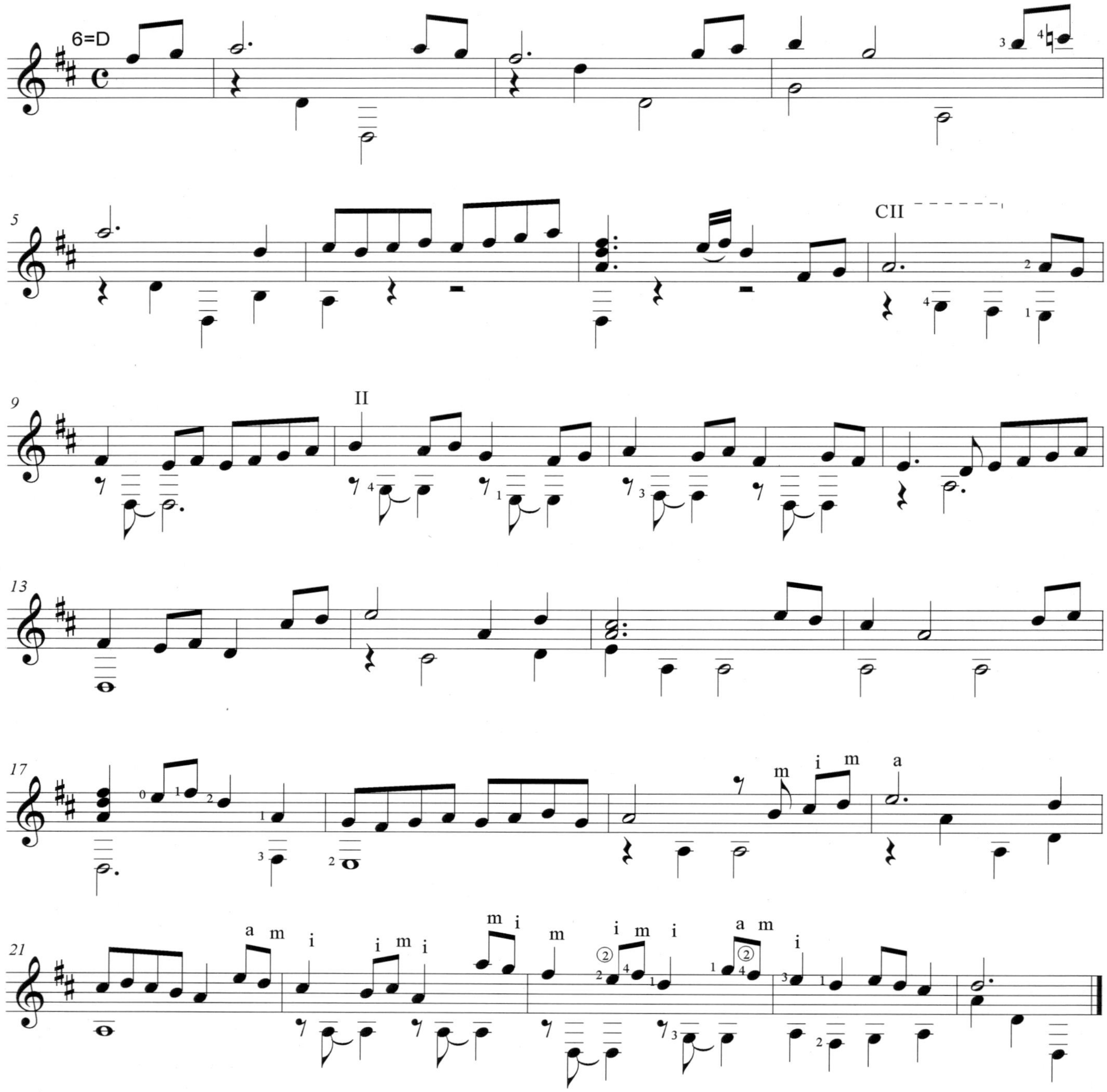

This page has been left blank to avoid an awkward page turn.

21. Bourée d'Avignon

Nicolas Vallet

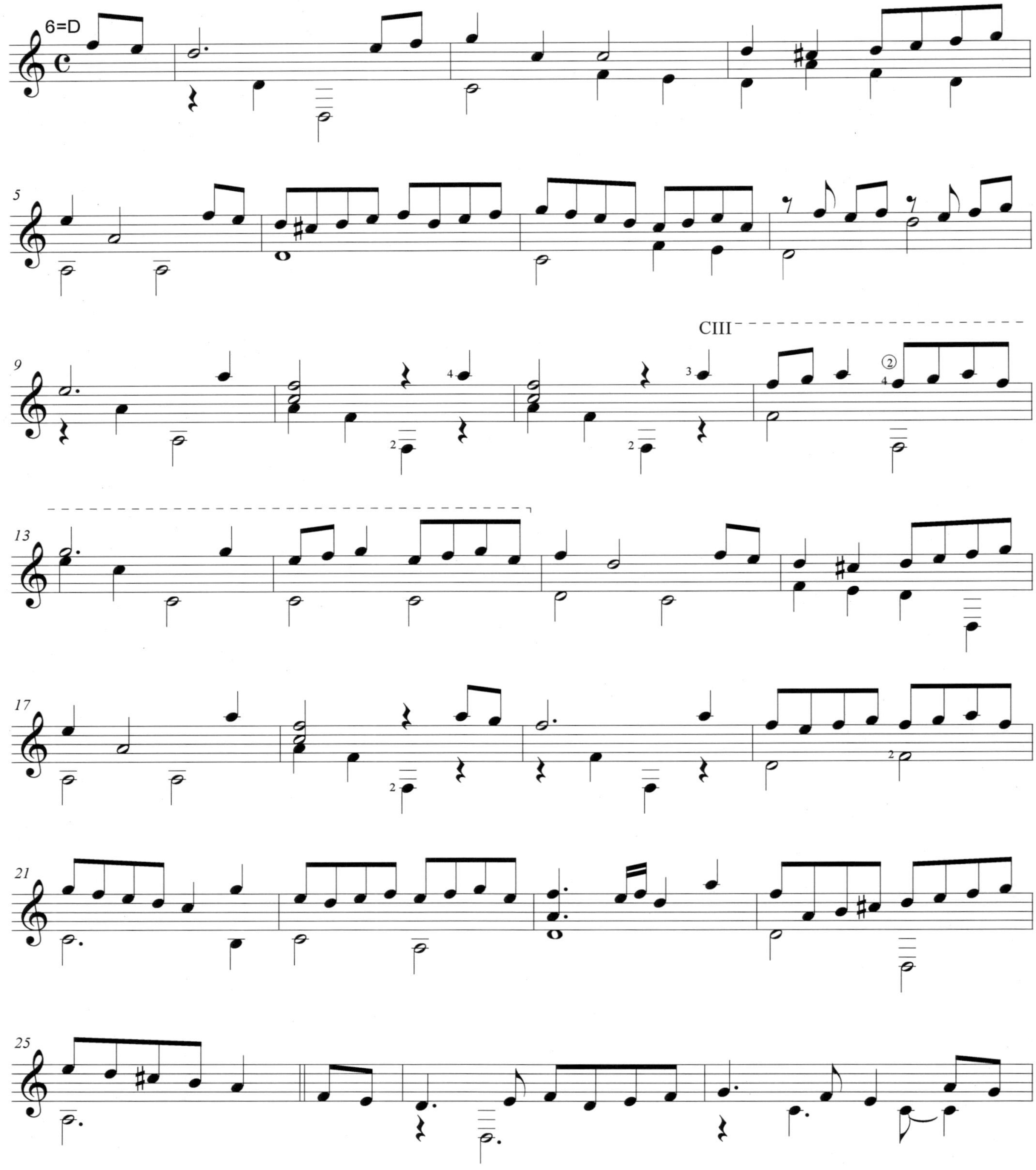

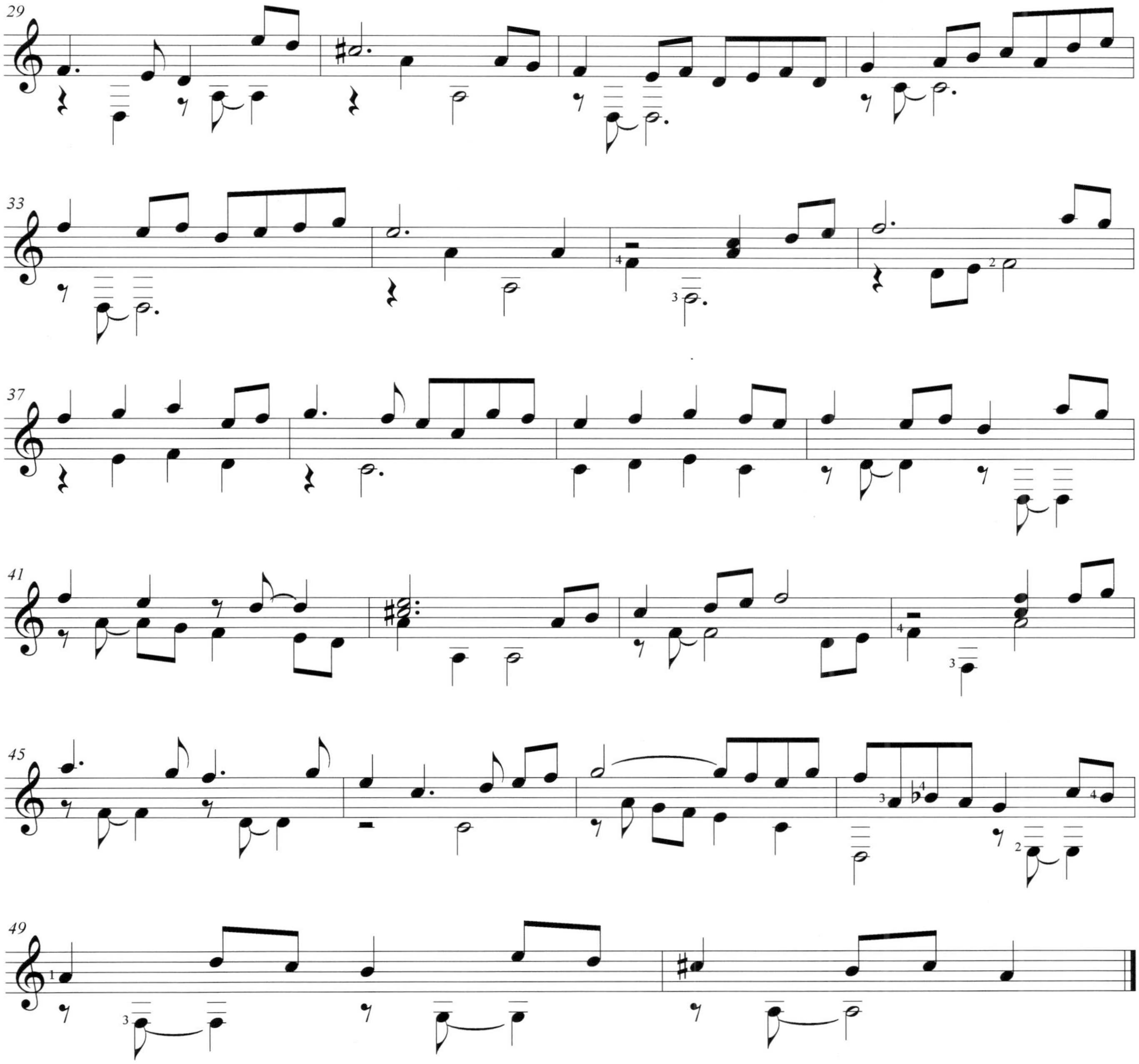
29
33
37
41
45
49

22. Fortune Angloise

Nicolas Vallet

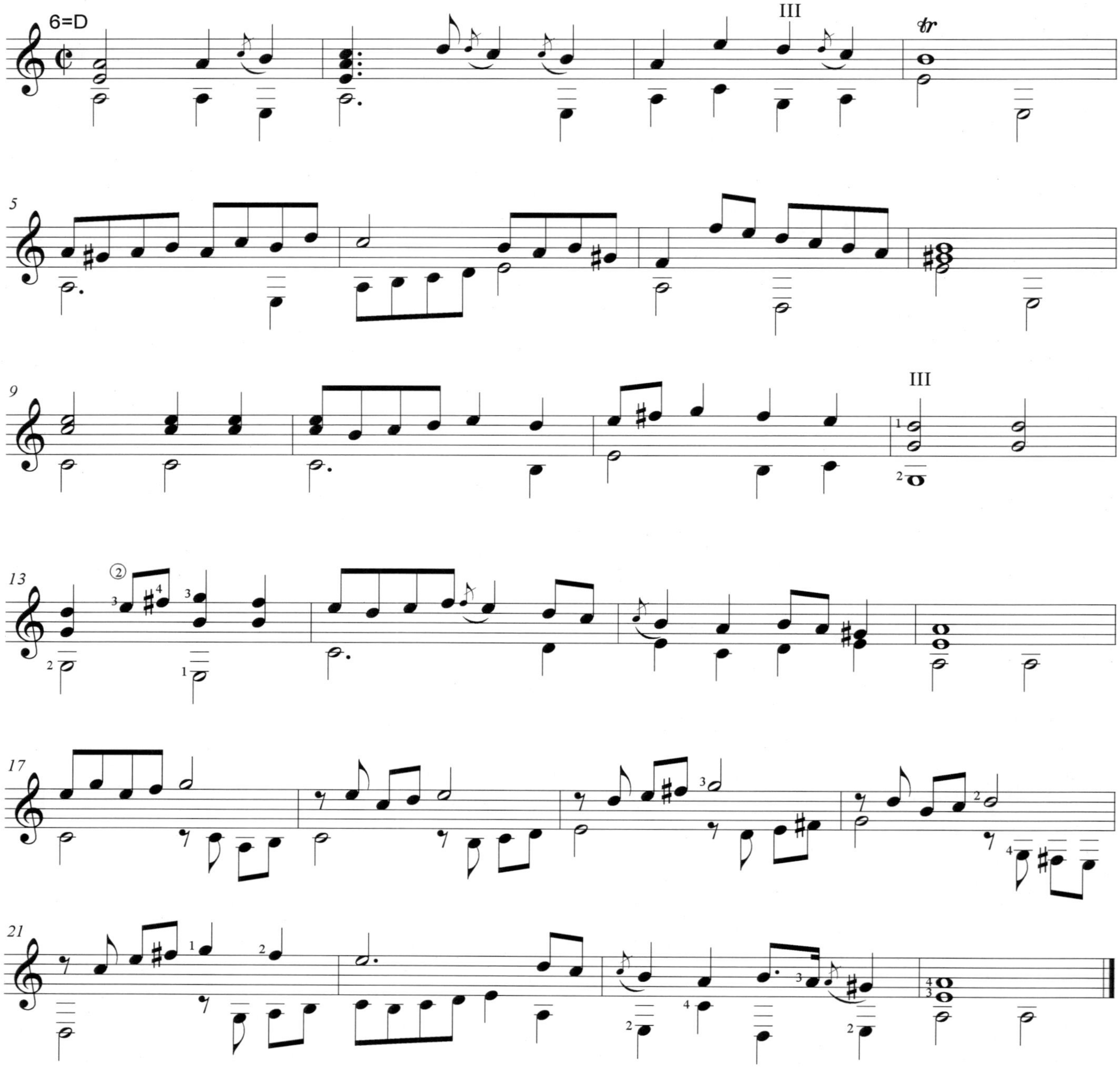

23. Slaep Soete Slaep

Nicolas Vallet

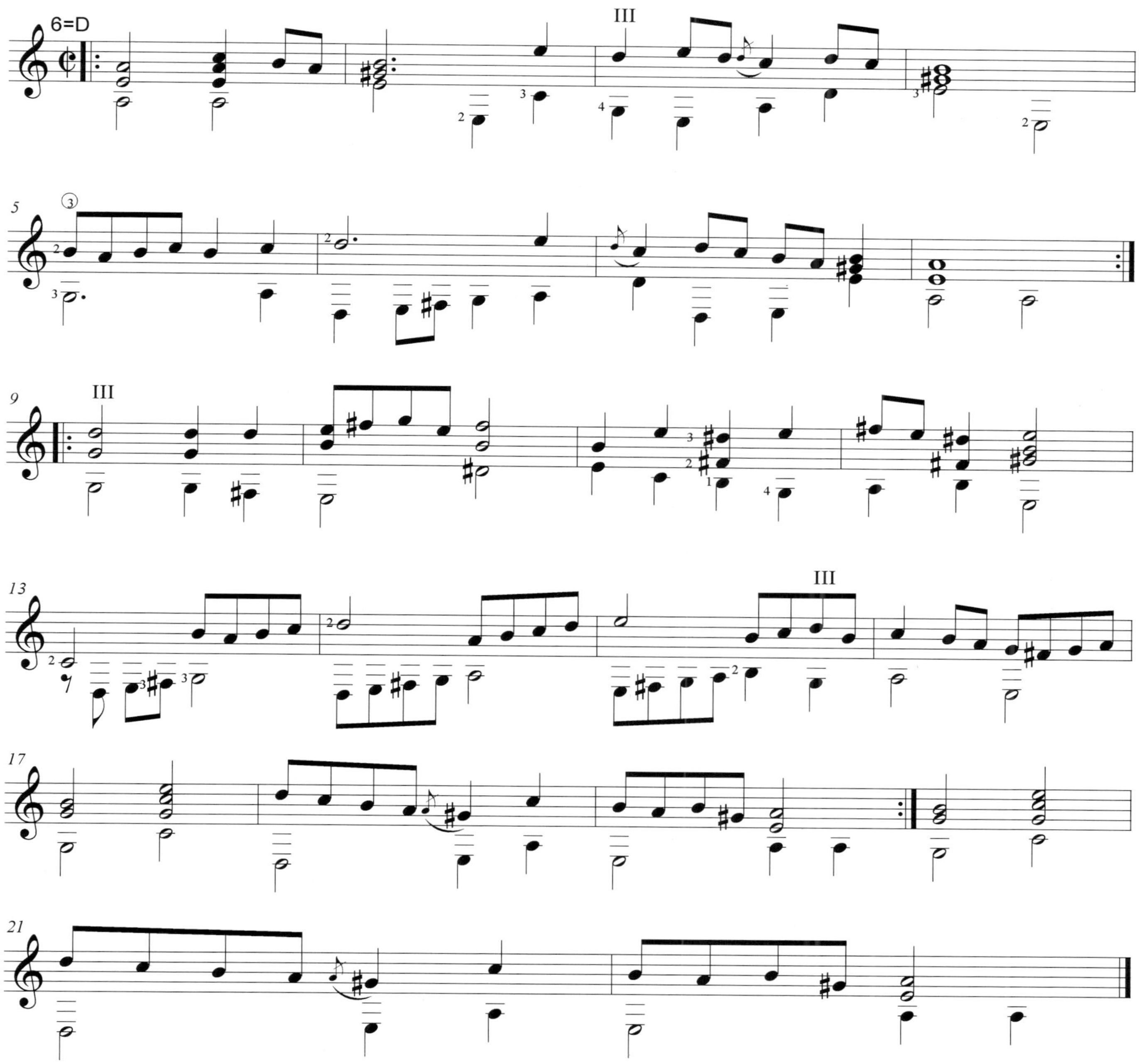

24. La Piccarde

Nicolas Vallet

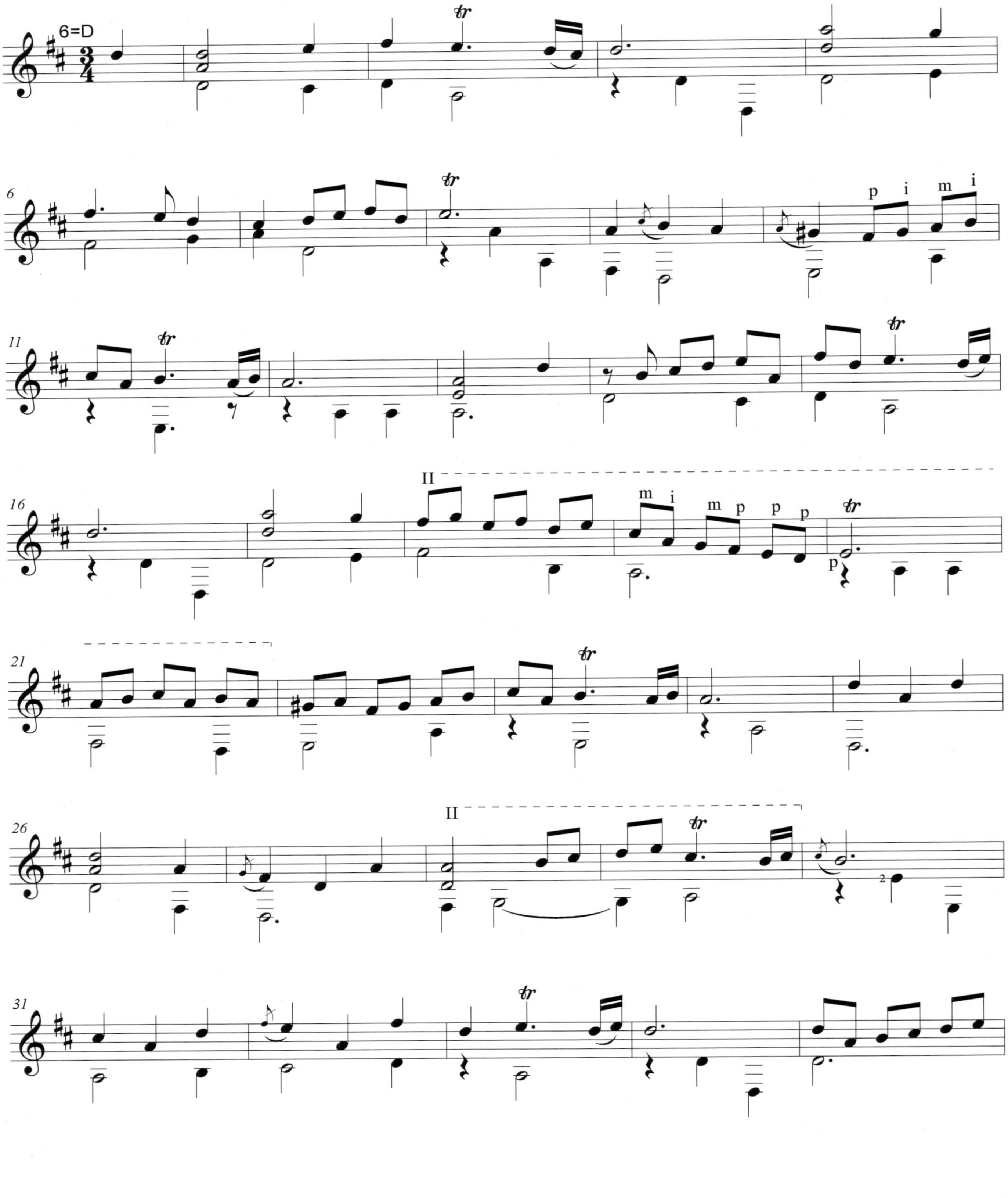

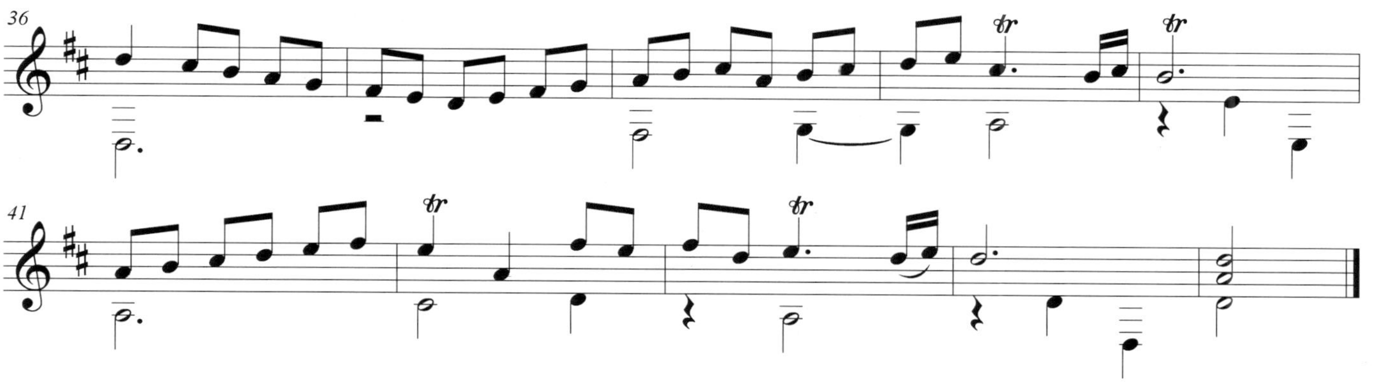
36
tr
tr
41
tr
tr

25. La Favorite

Nicolas Vallet

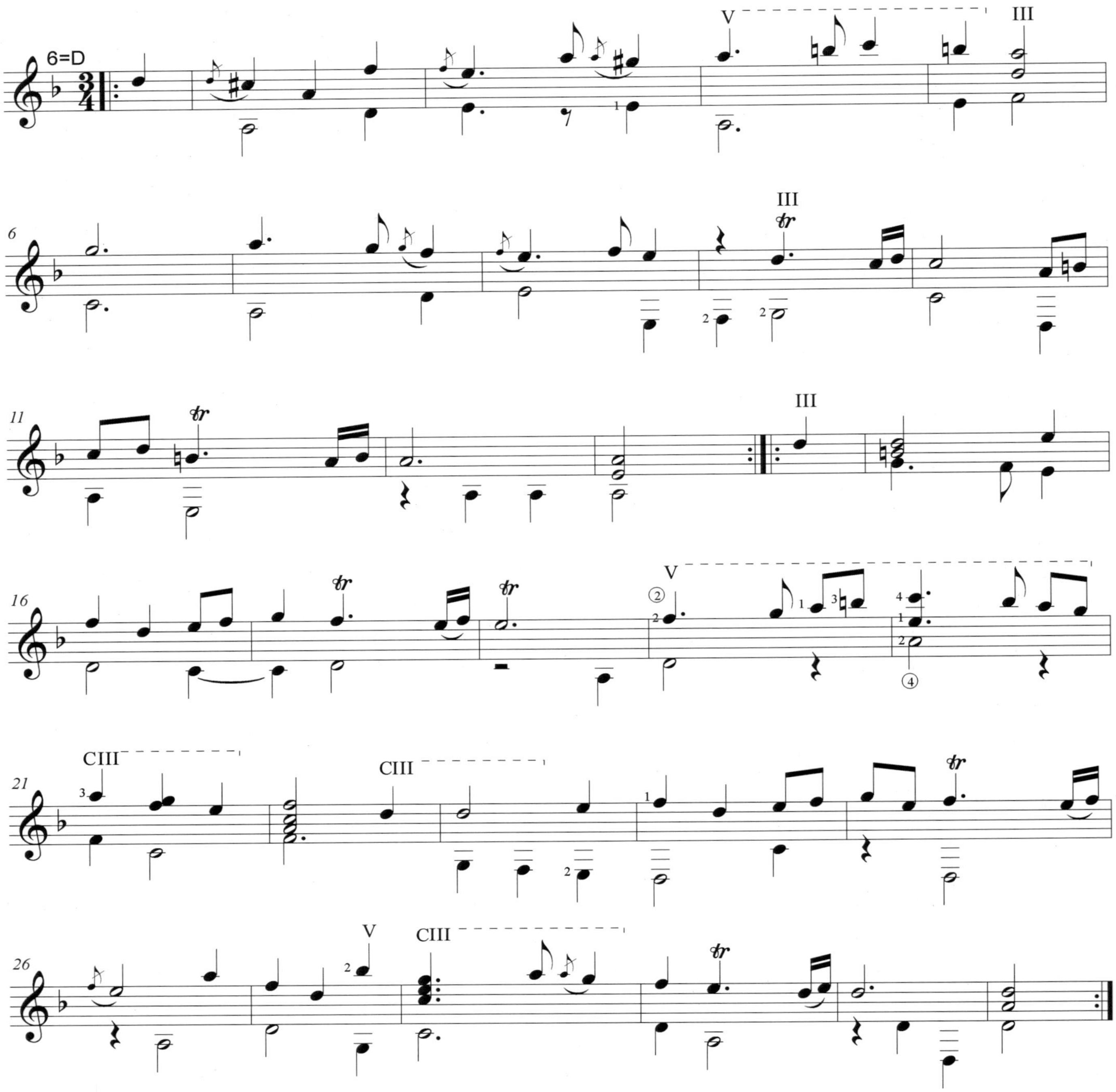

26. Ballet

Nicolas Vallet

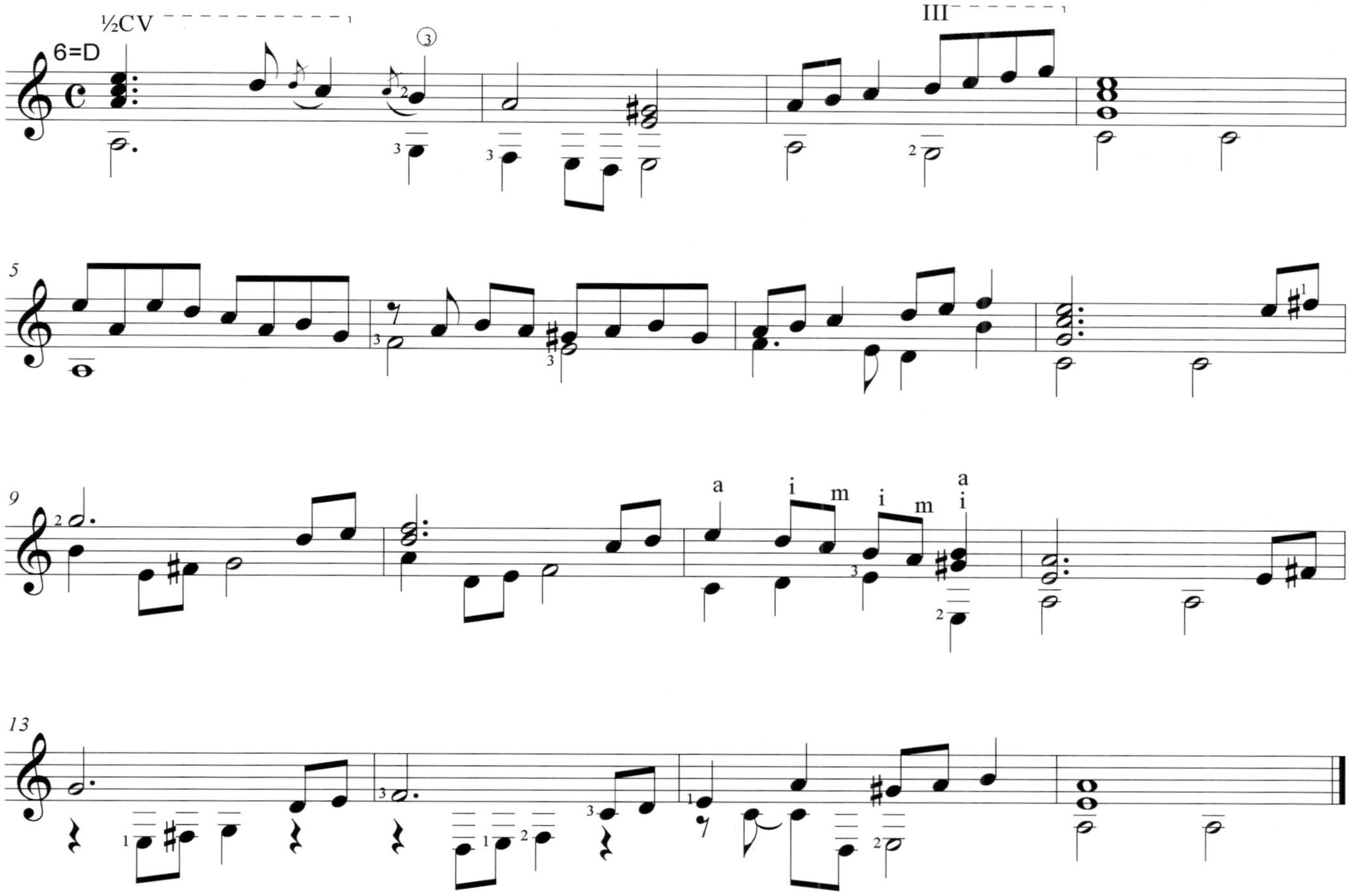

27. Ballet

Nicolas Vallet

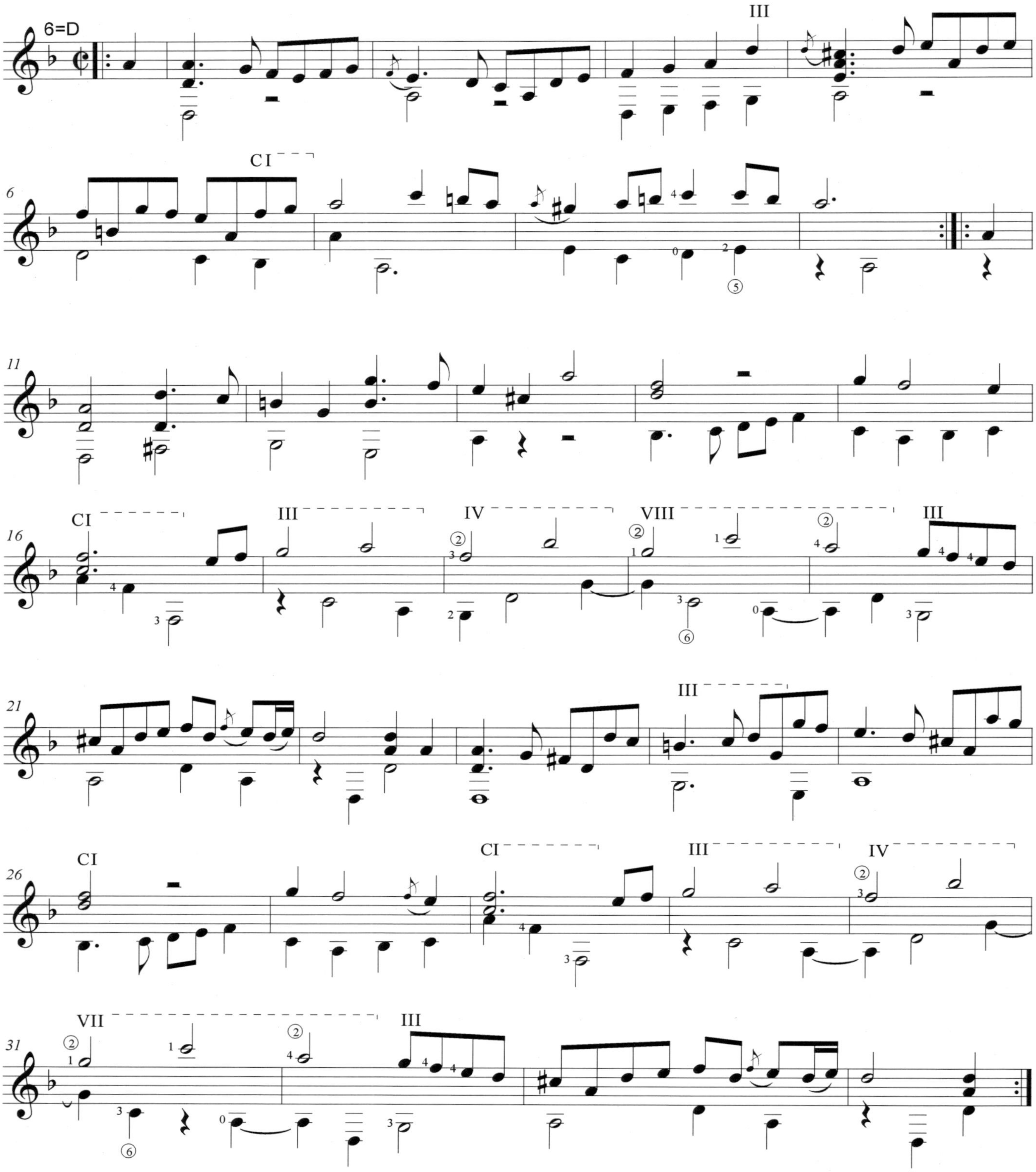

28. Ballet

Nicolas Vallet

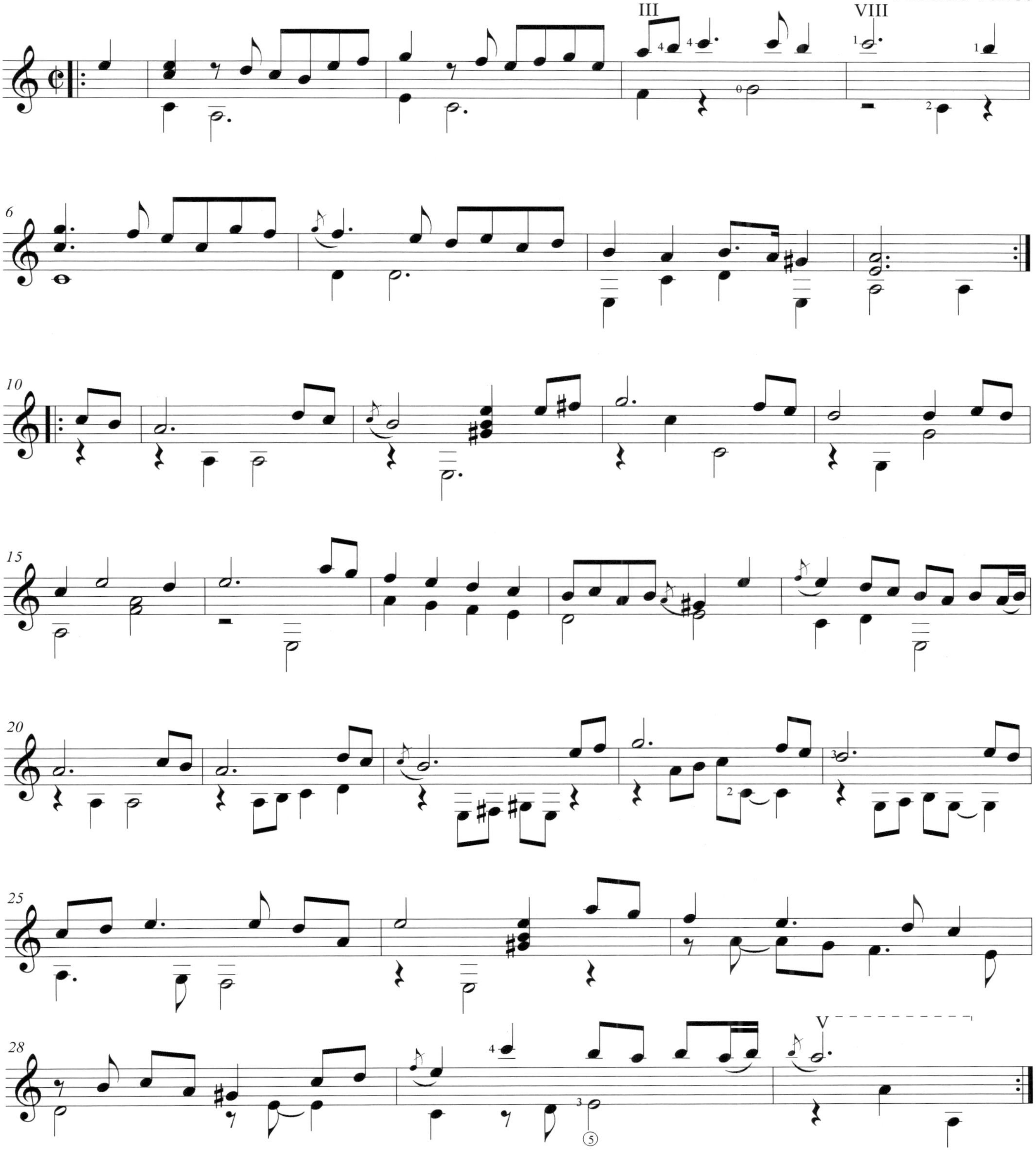

29. Ballet

Nicolas Vallet

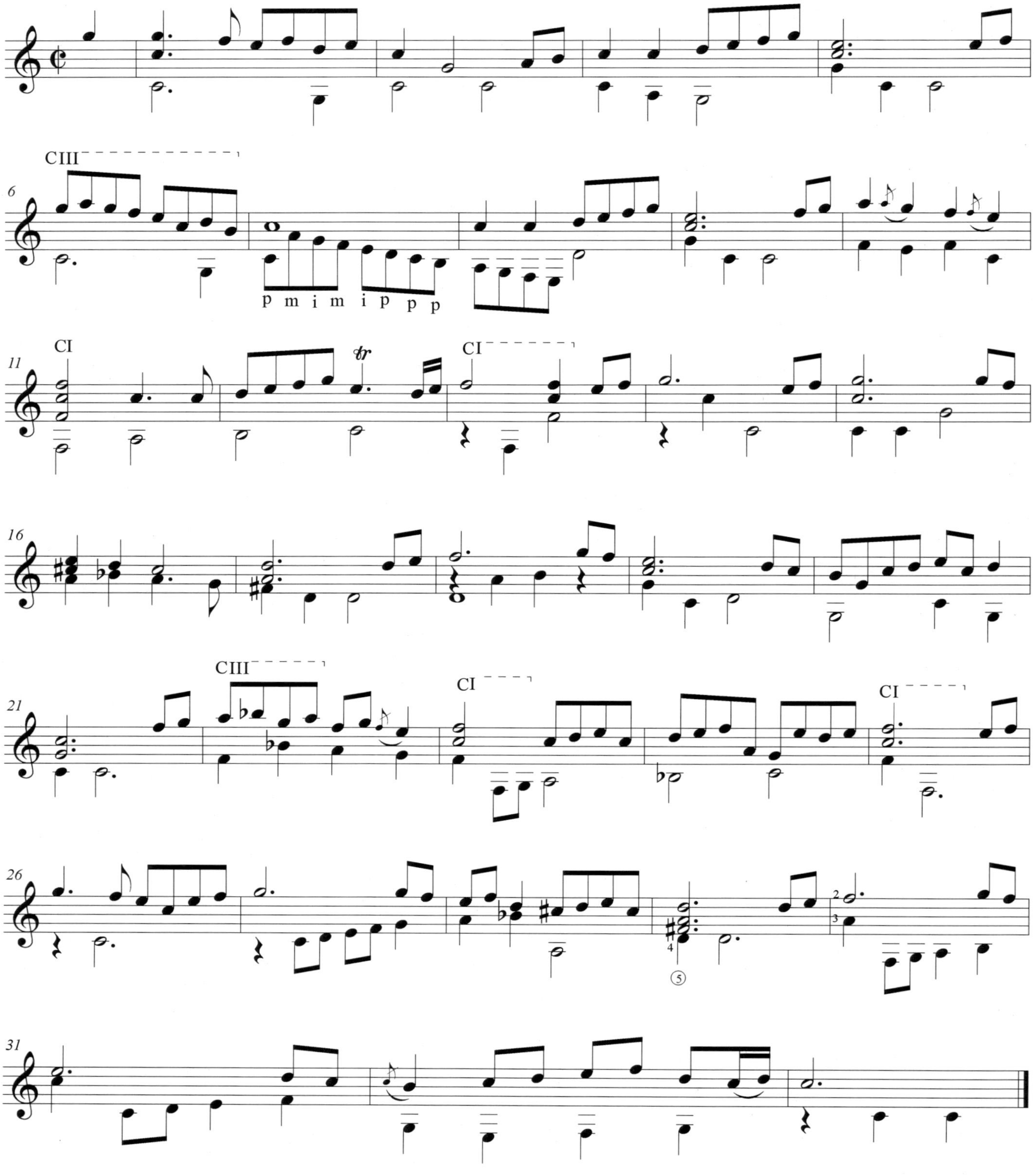

30. Ballet

Nicolas Vallet

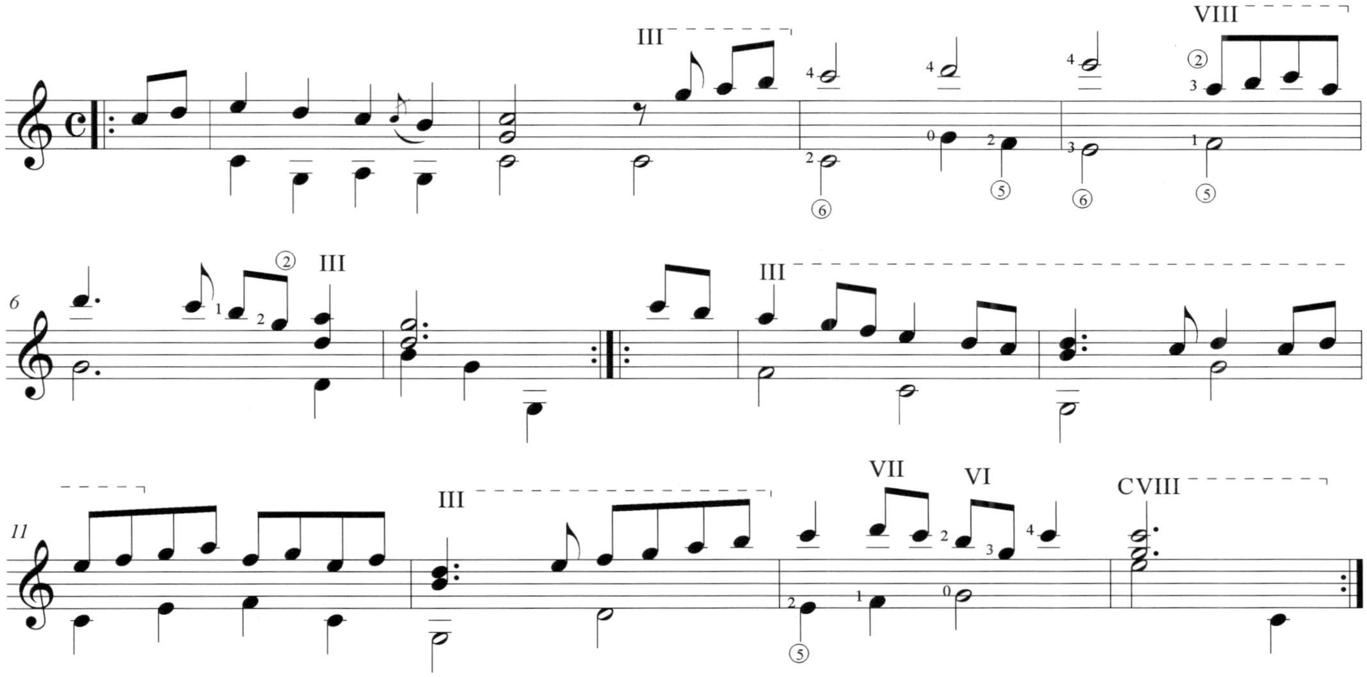

31. Ballet

Nicolas Vallet

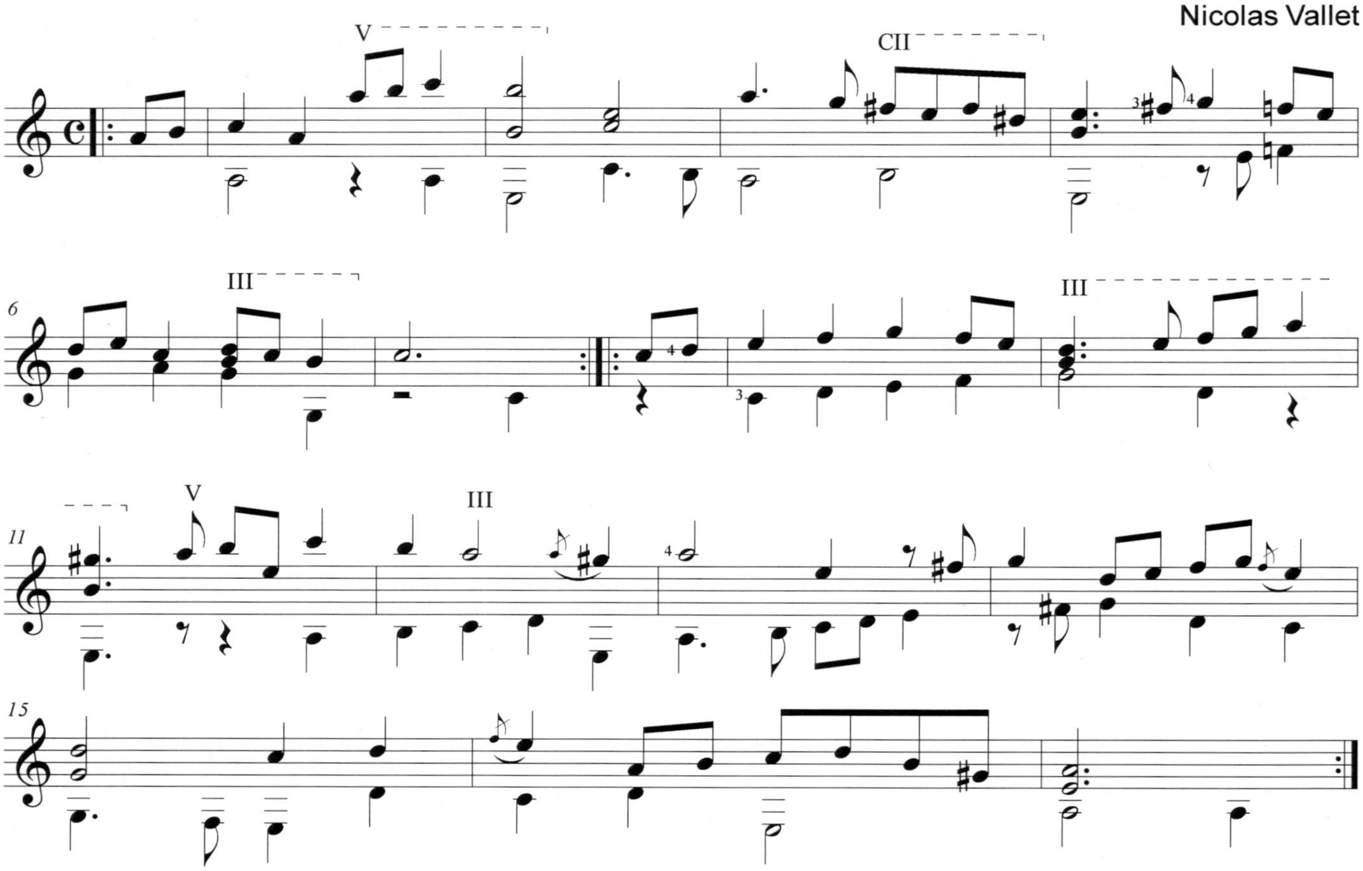

32. Ballet des Queux

Nicolas Vallet

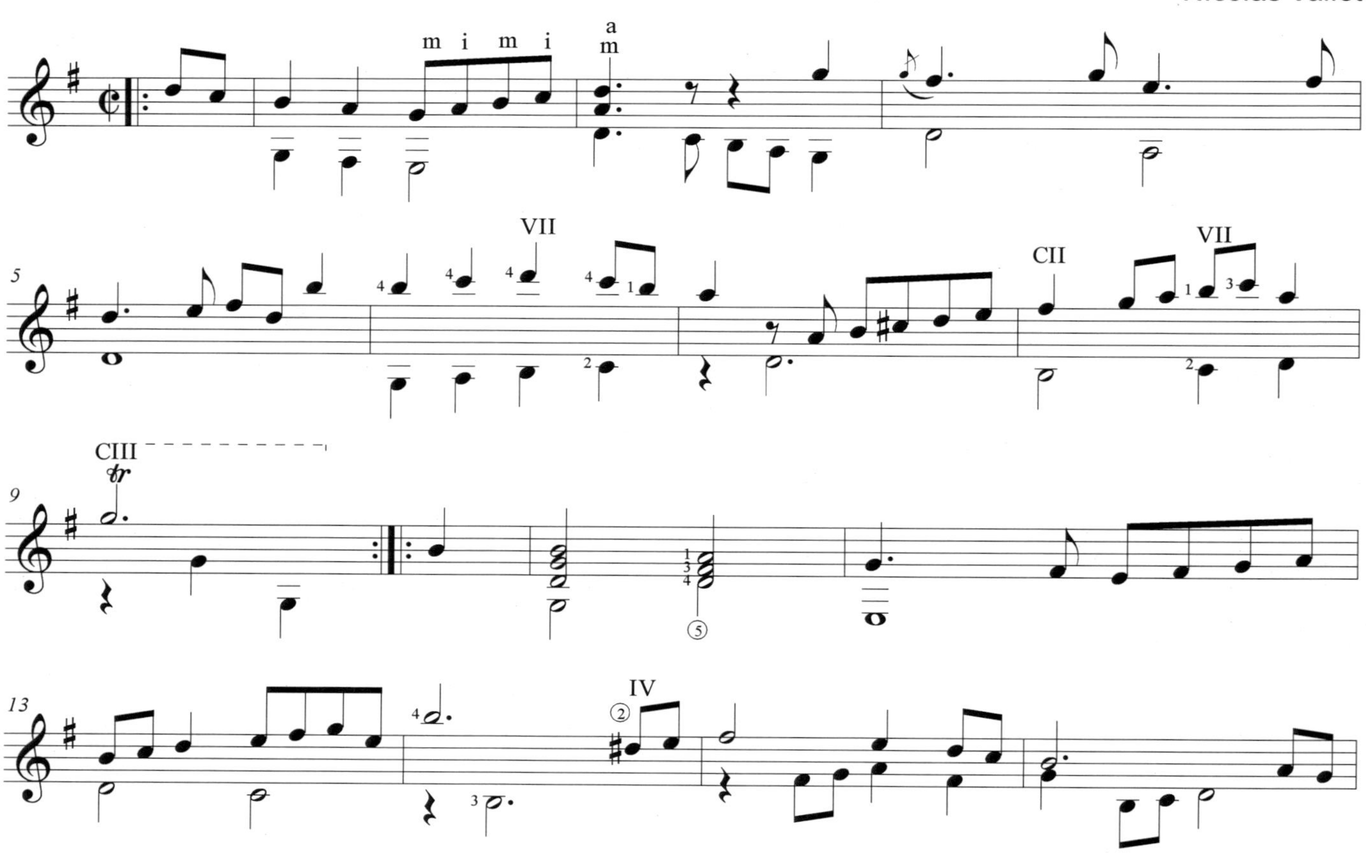

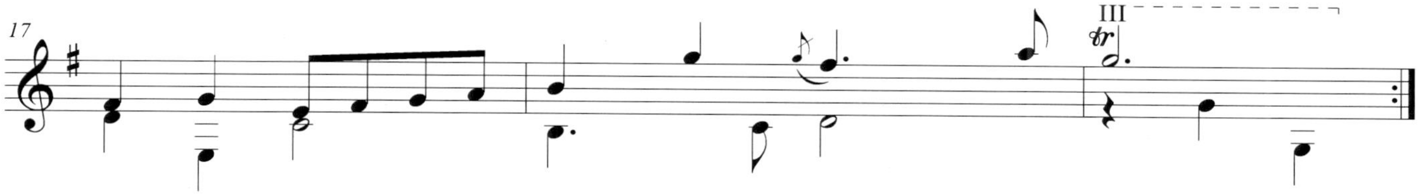

33. Gaillarde de la Passemeze

Nicolas Vallet

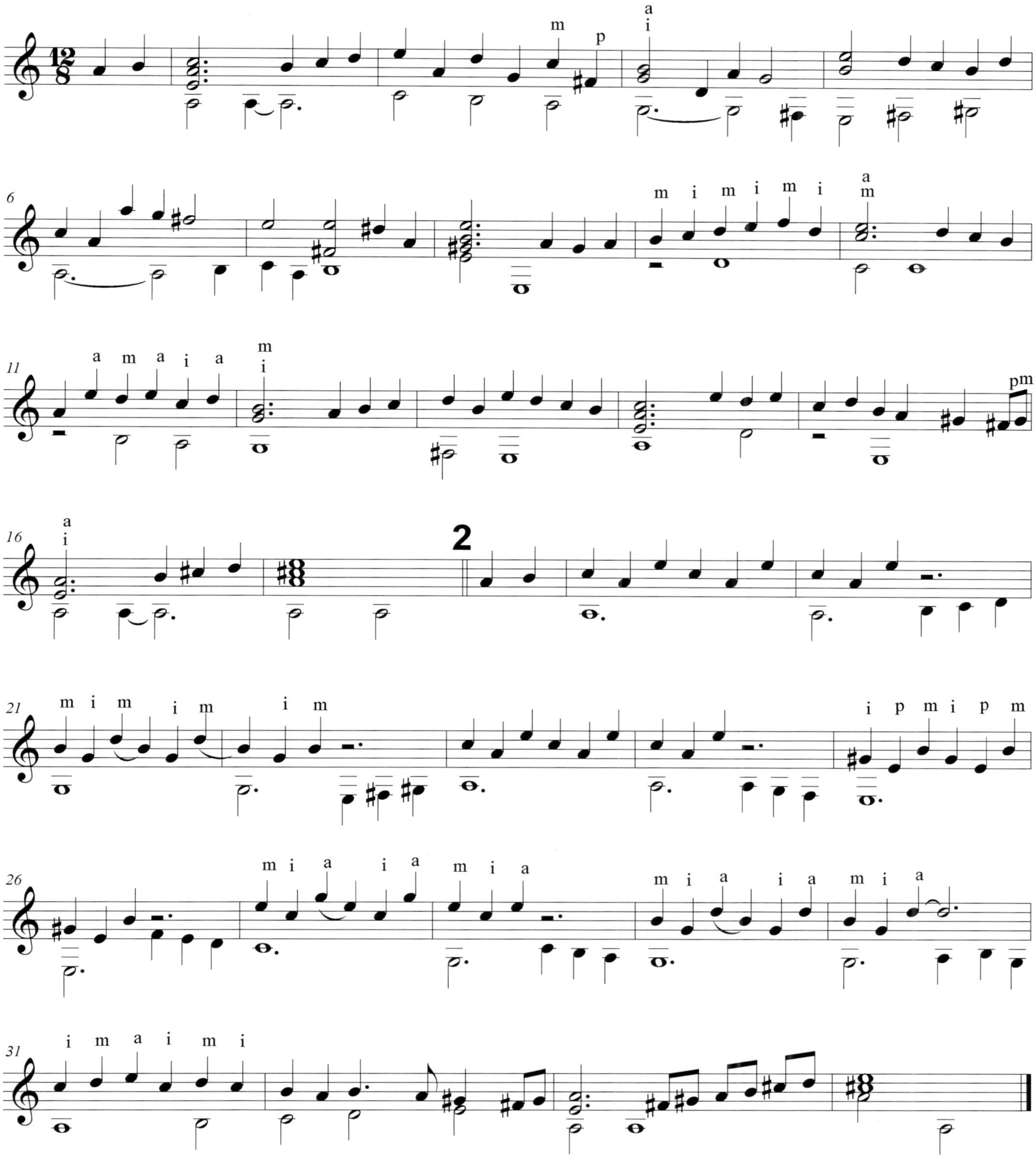

34. Courante

Nicolas Vallet

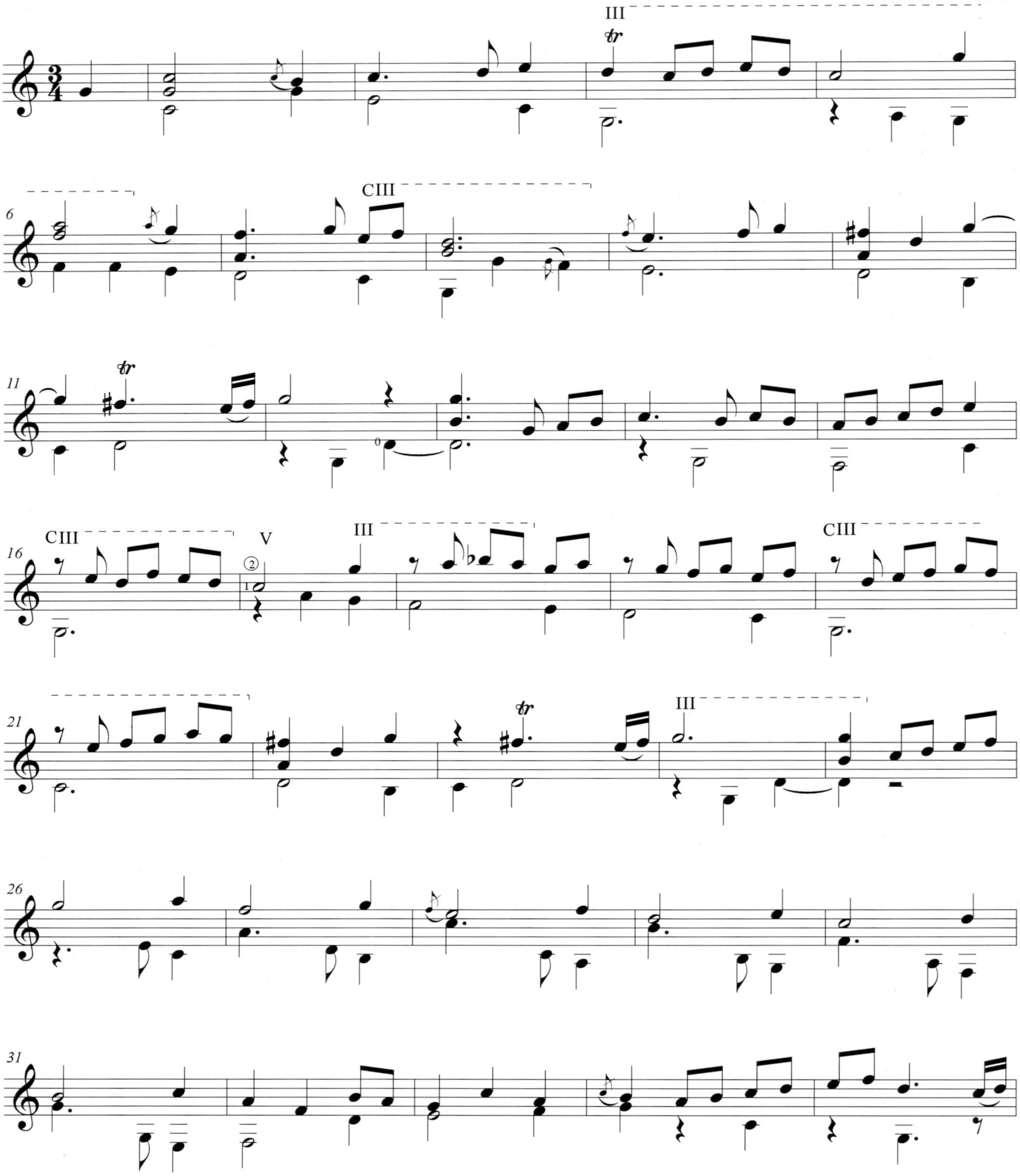

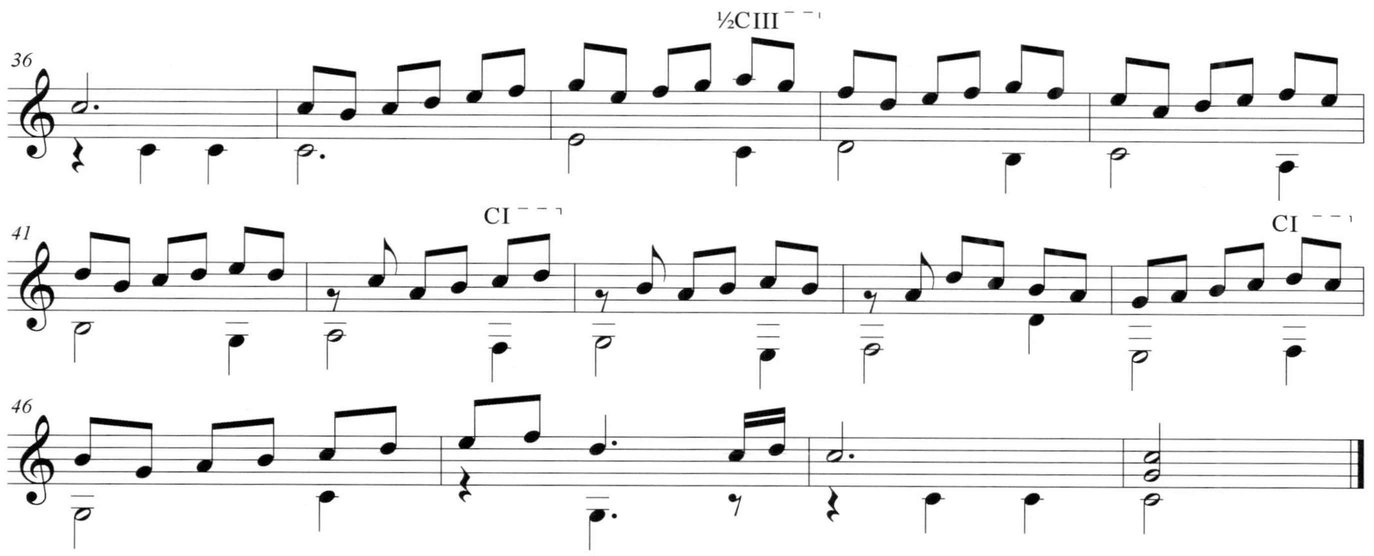
½CIII
CI
CI

35. Courante

Nicolas Vallet

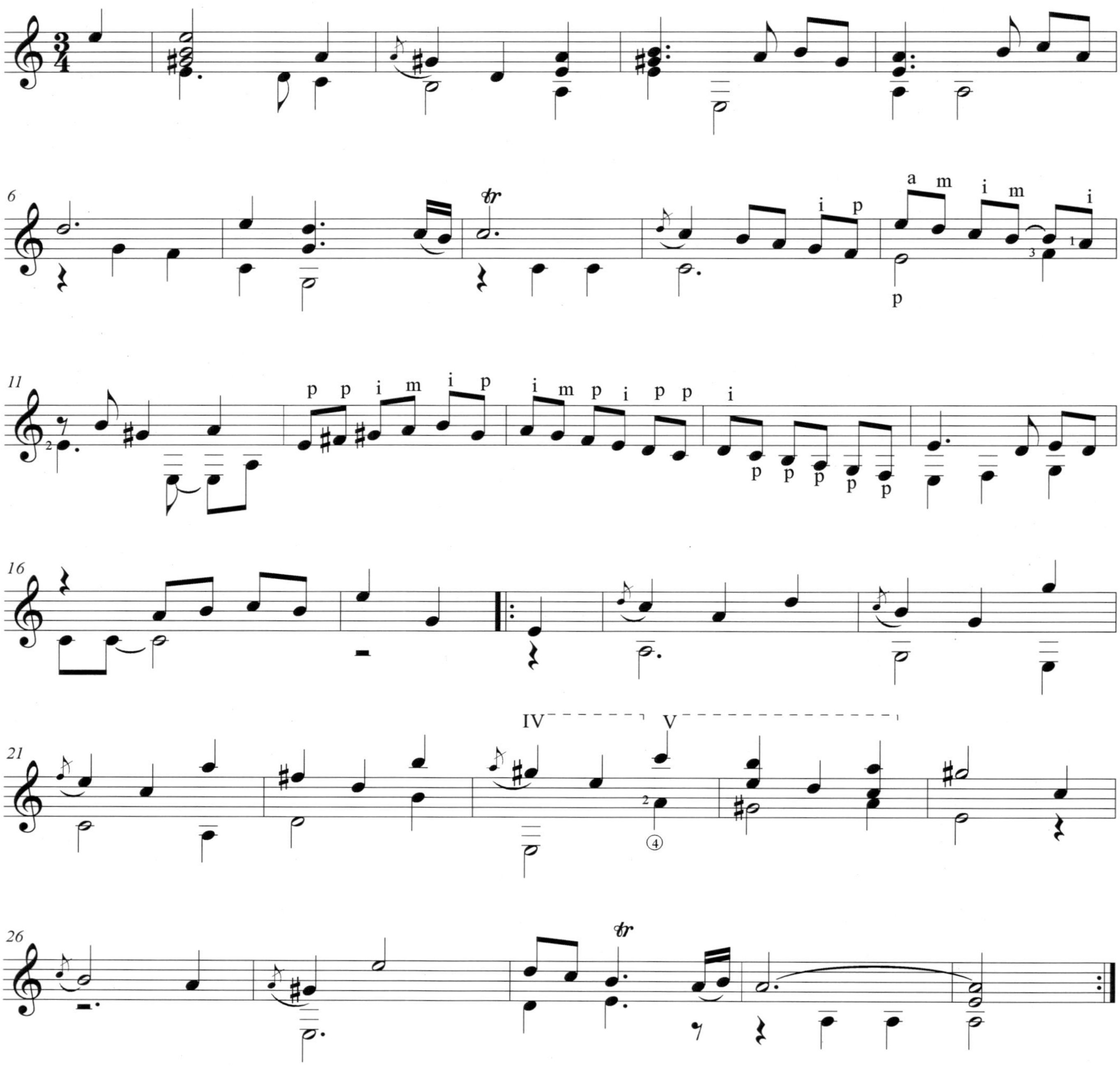

This page has been left blank to avoid an awkward page turn.

36. Courante

Nicolas Vallet

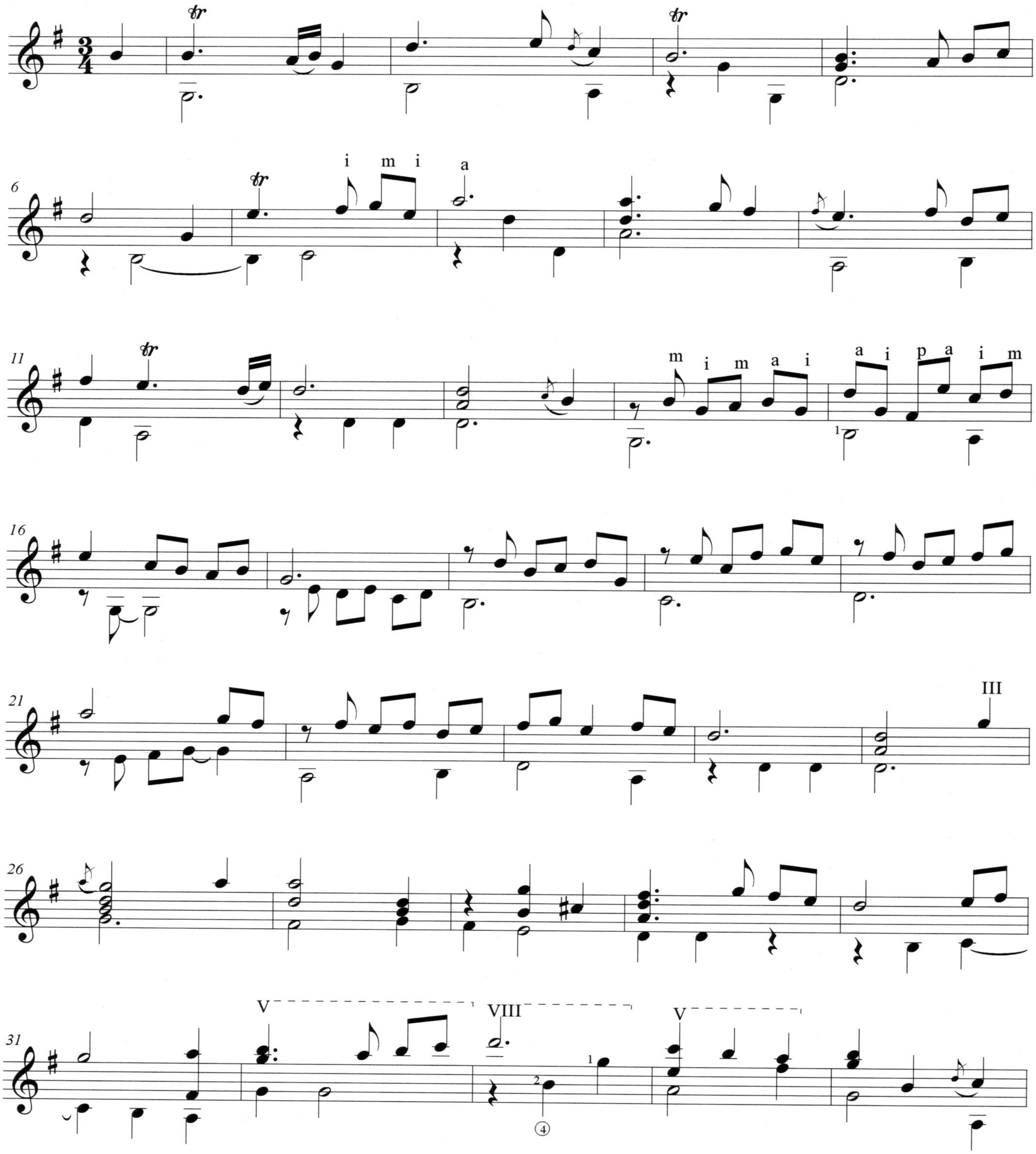

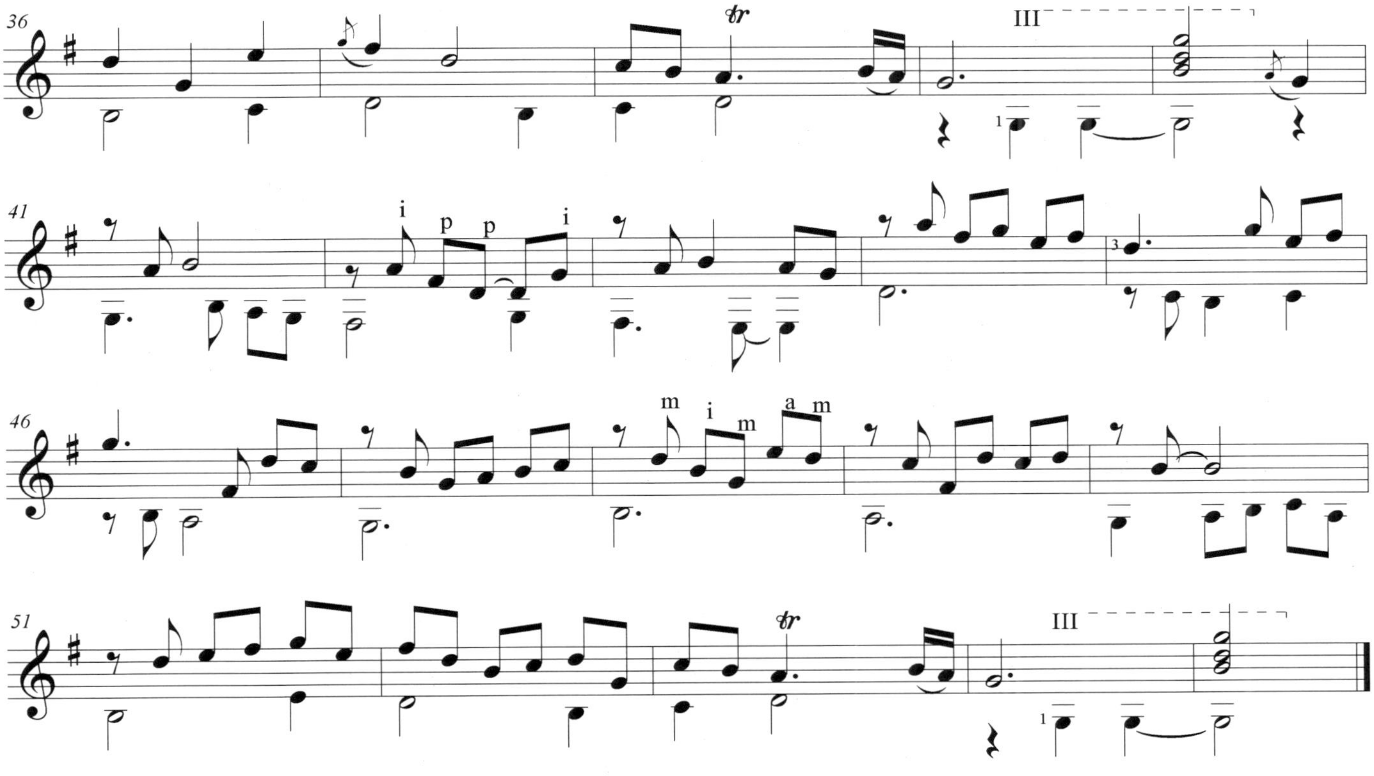
36
tr
III
41
i p p i
46
m i m a m
51
tr
III

37. Courante

Nicolas Vallet

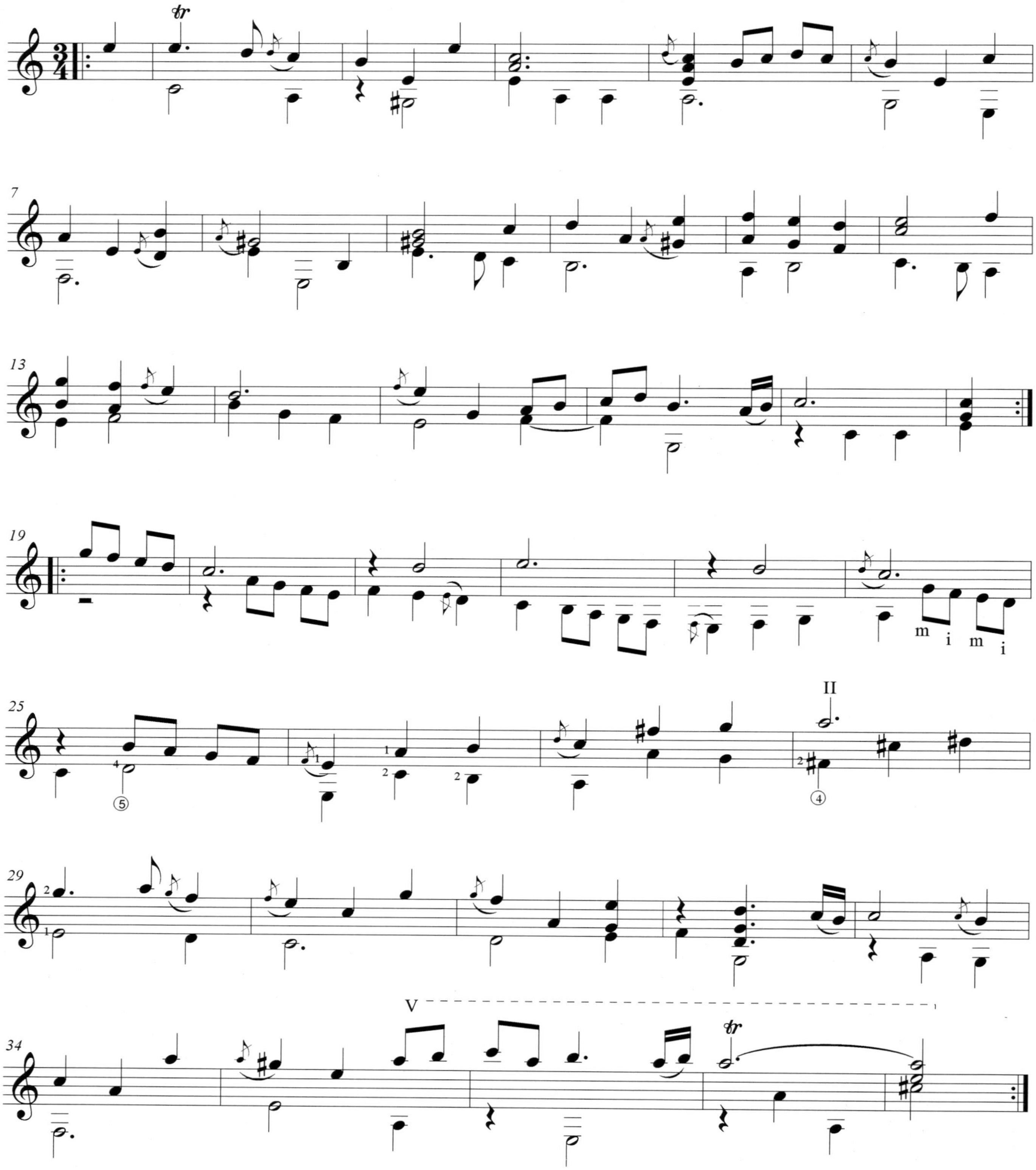

38. Courante de Mars

Nicolas Vallet

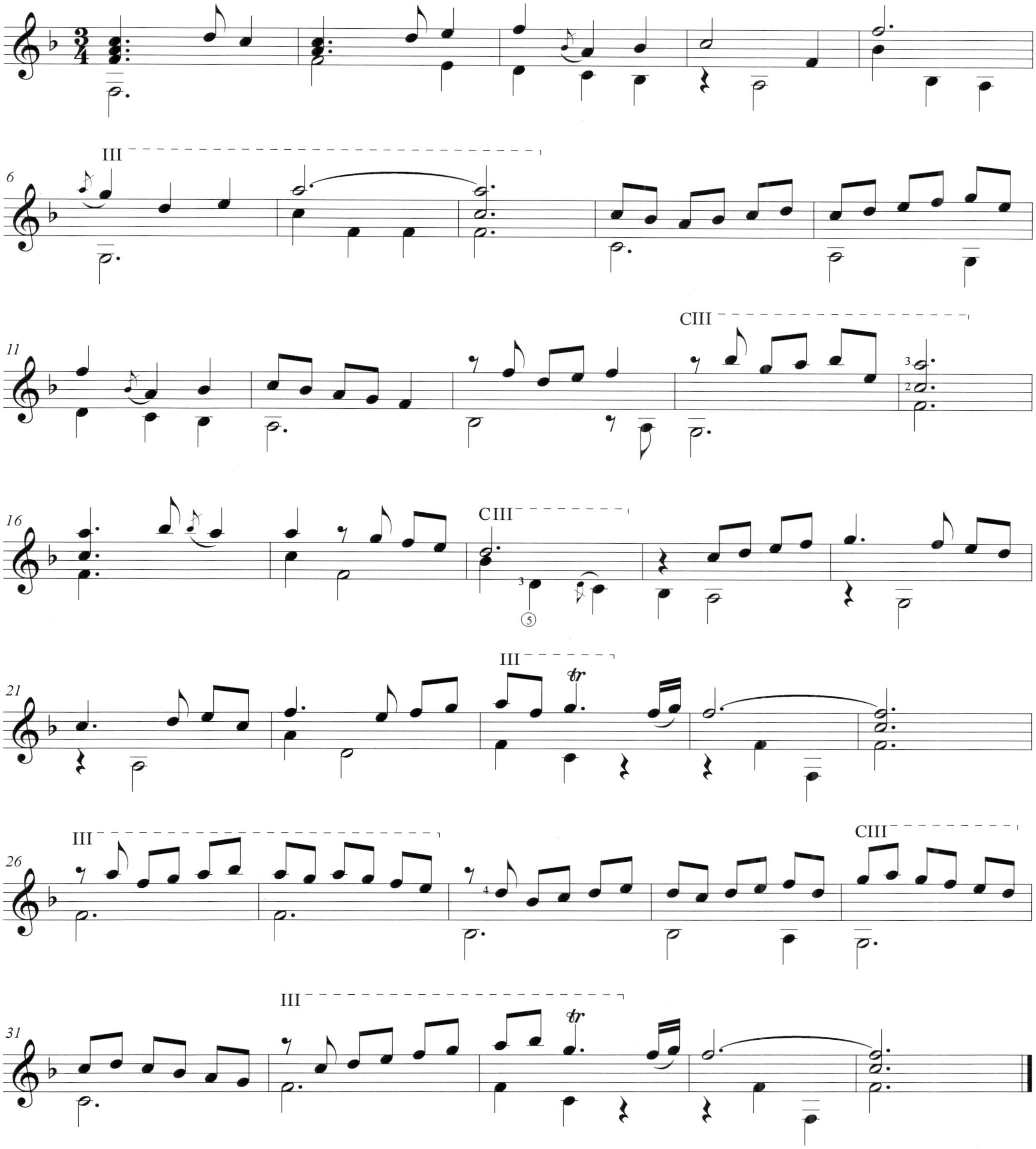

39. Courante de Mars

Nicolas Vallet

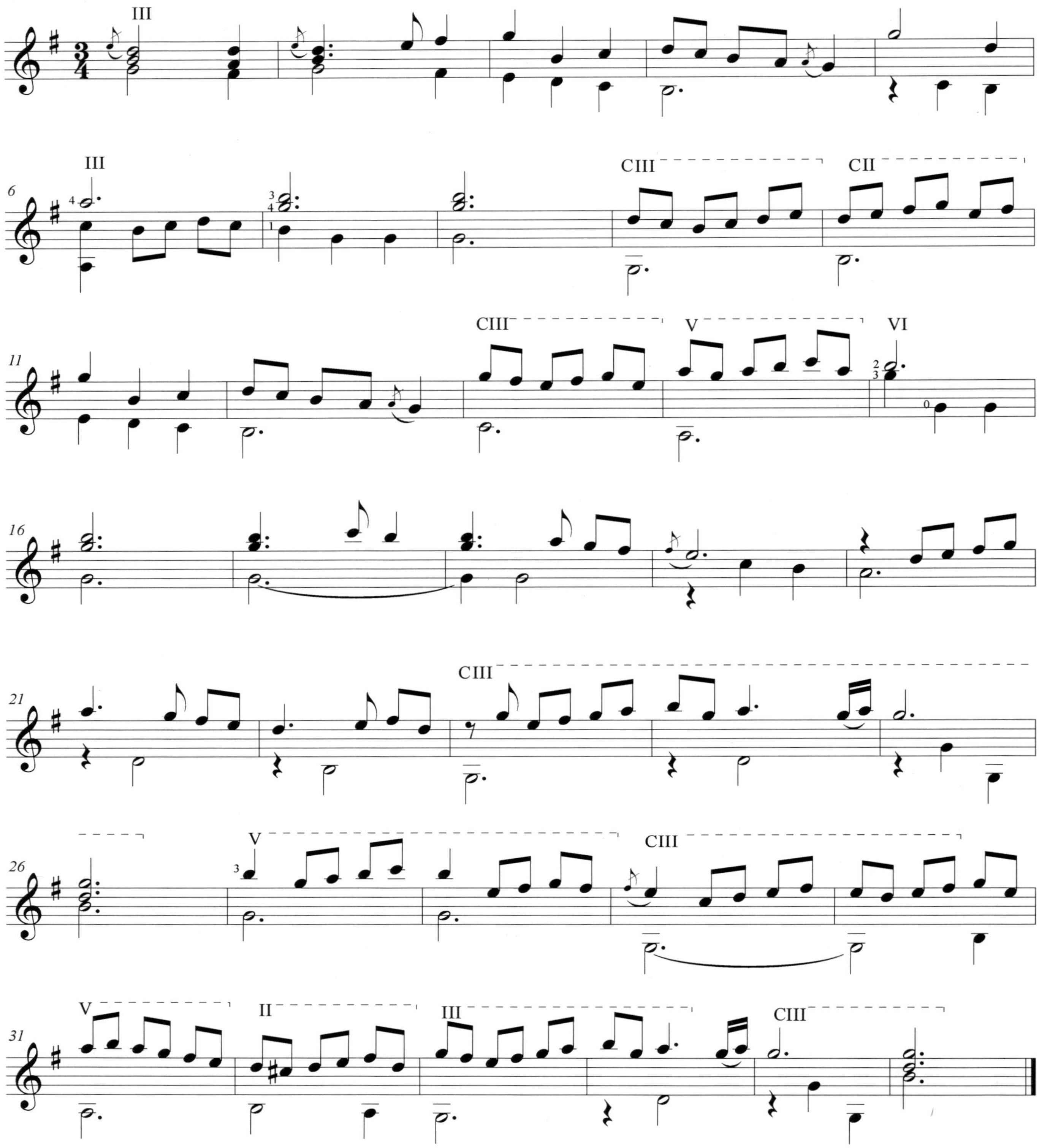

40. Suite

Nicolas Vallet

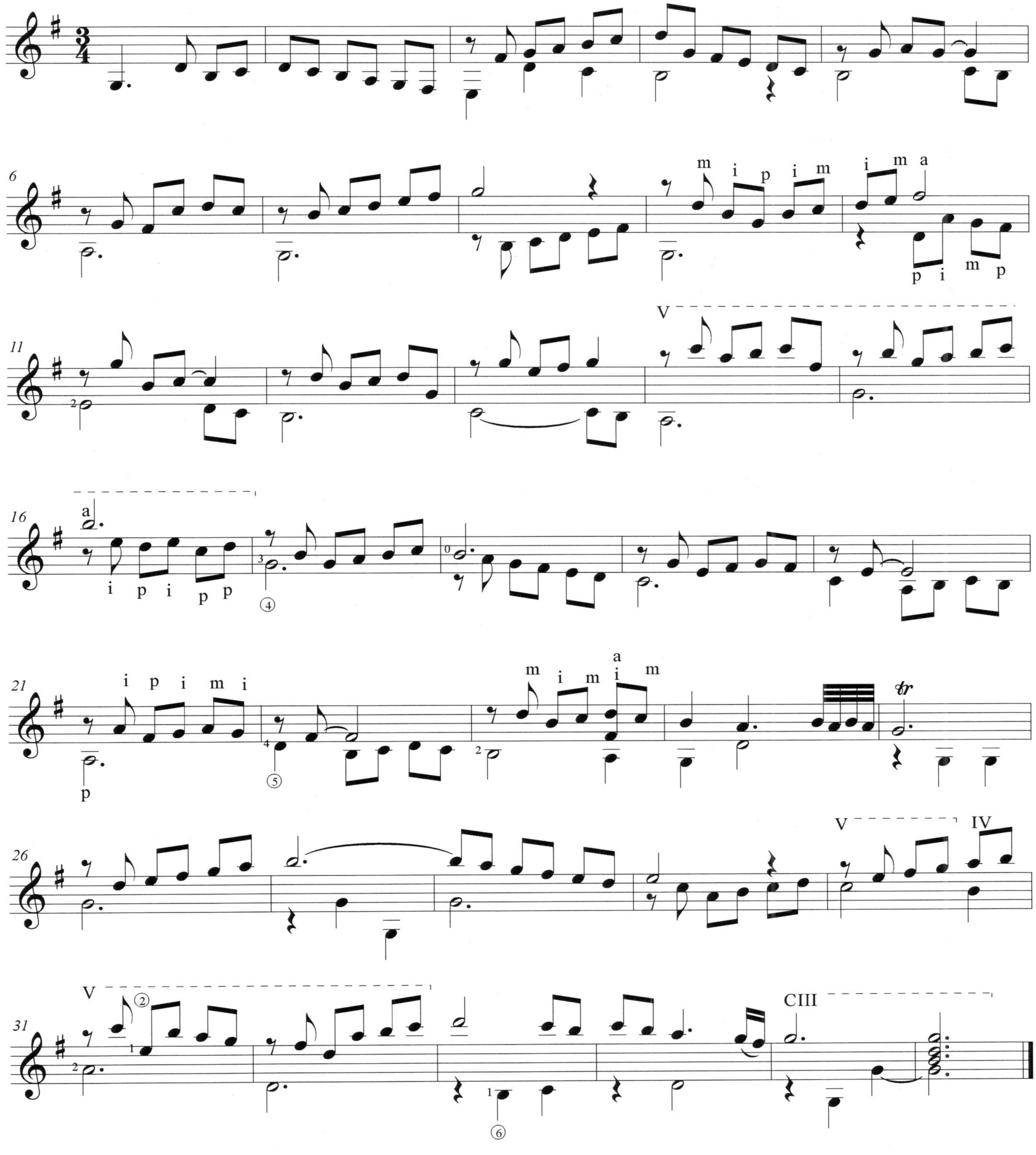

41. Pavanne de Espagne

Nicolas Vallet

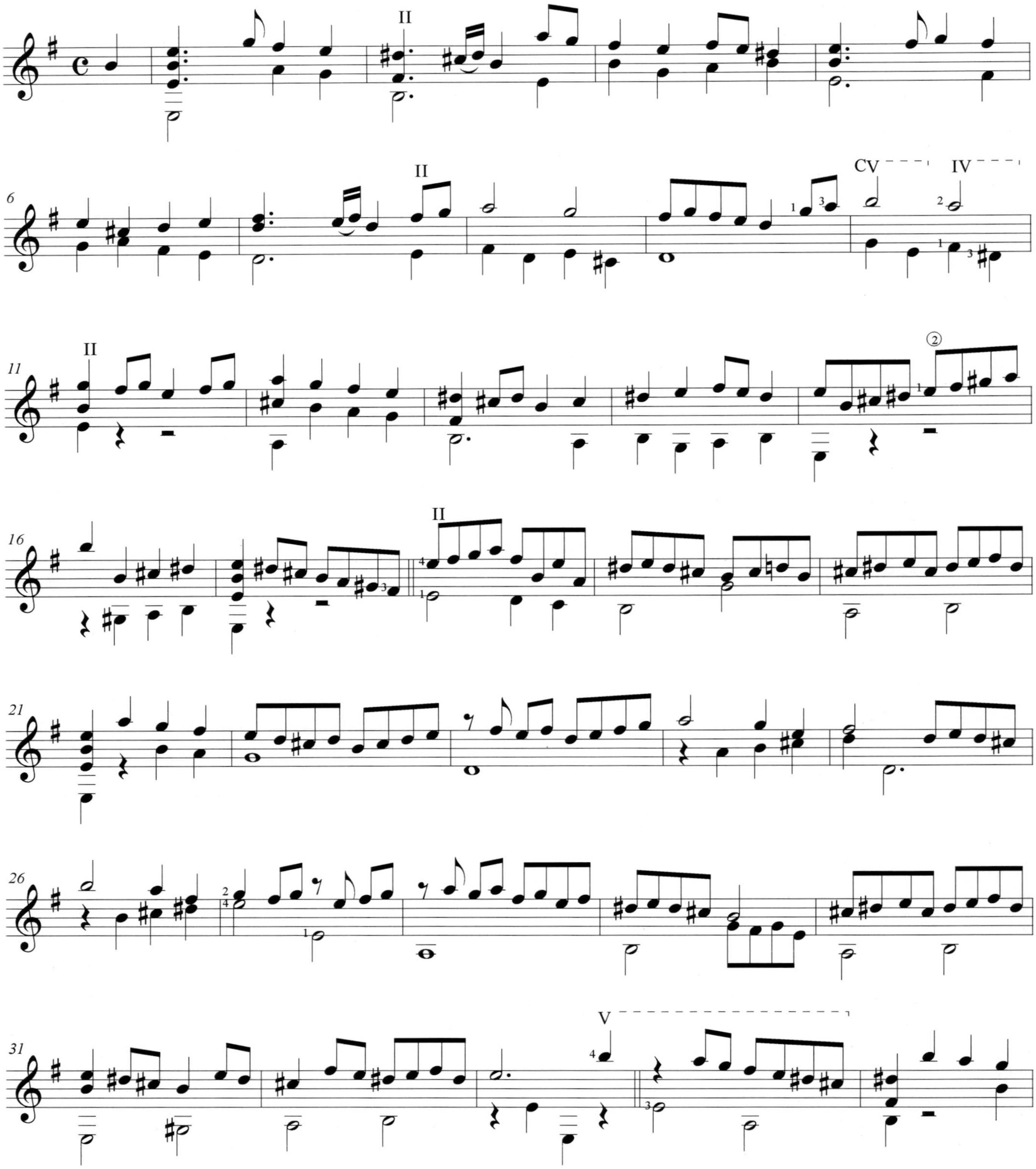

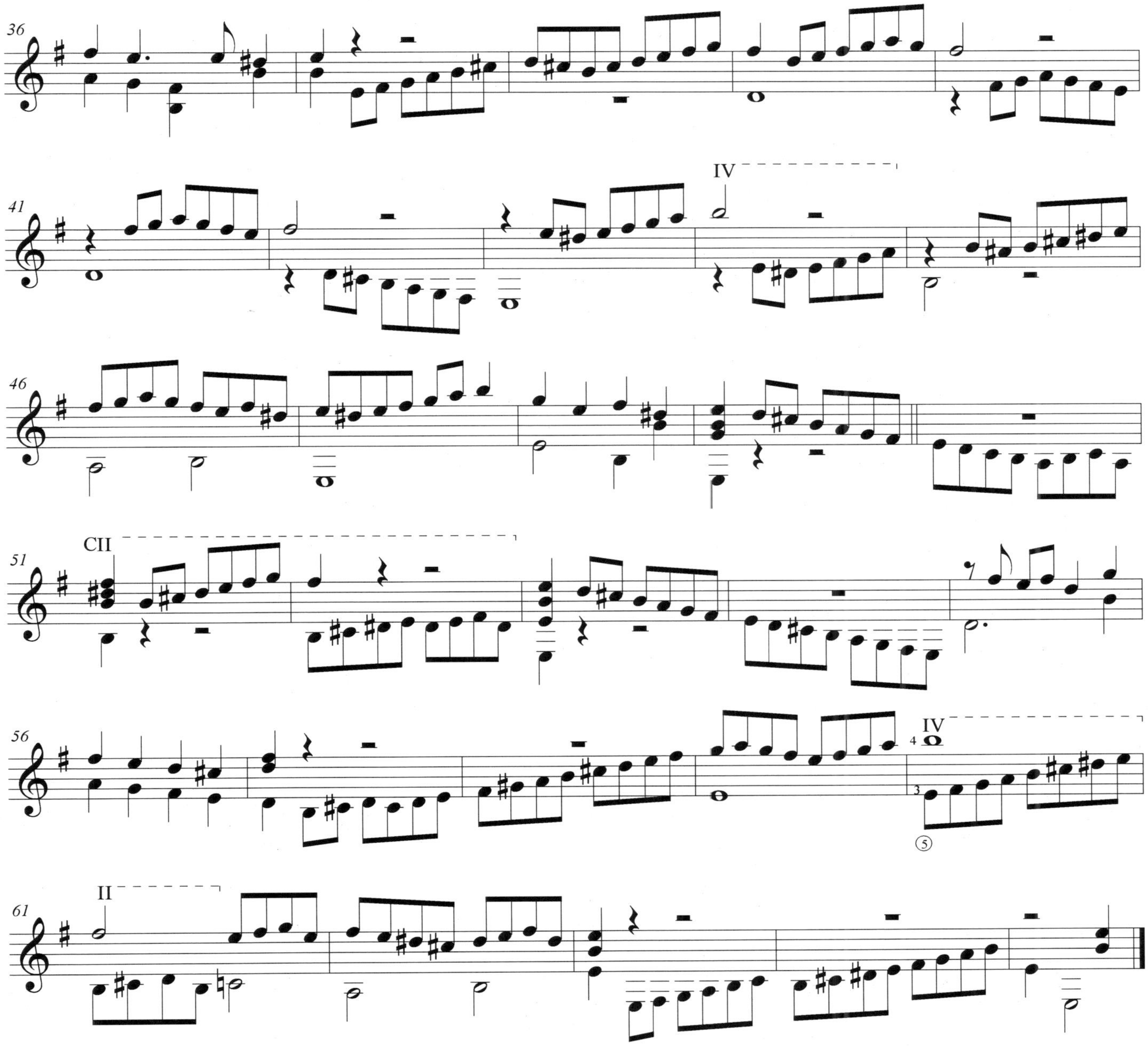
36
41
IV
46
51
CII
56
IV
61
II

42. Susannesco

Nicolas Vallet

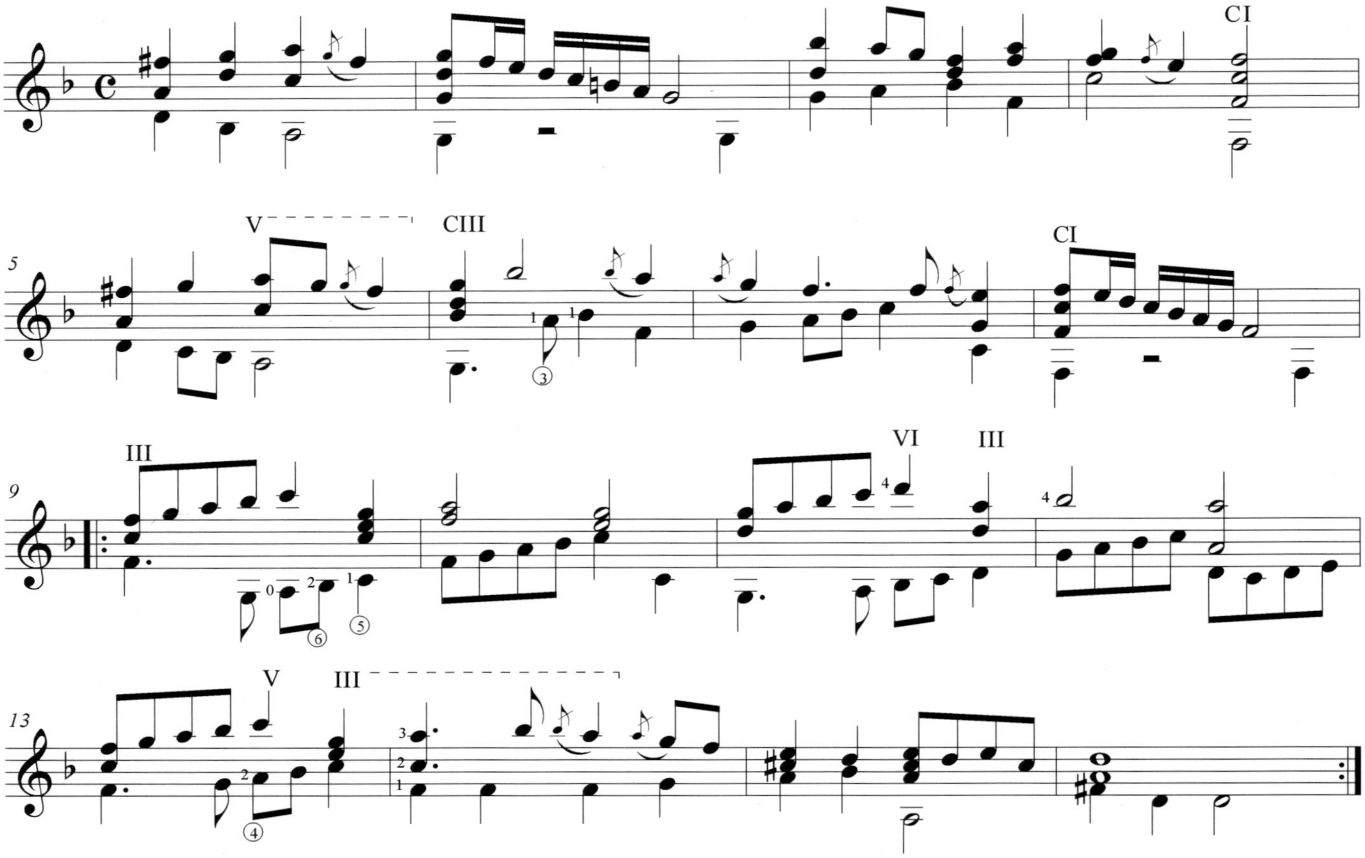

43. L'éscossoise

Nicolas Vallet

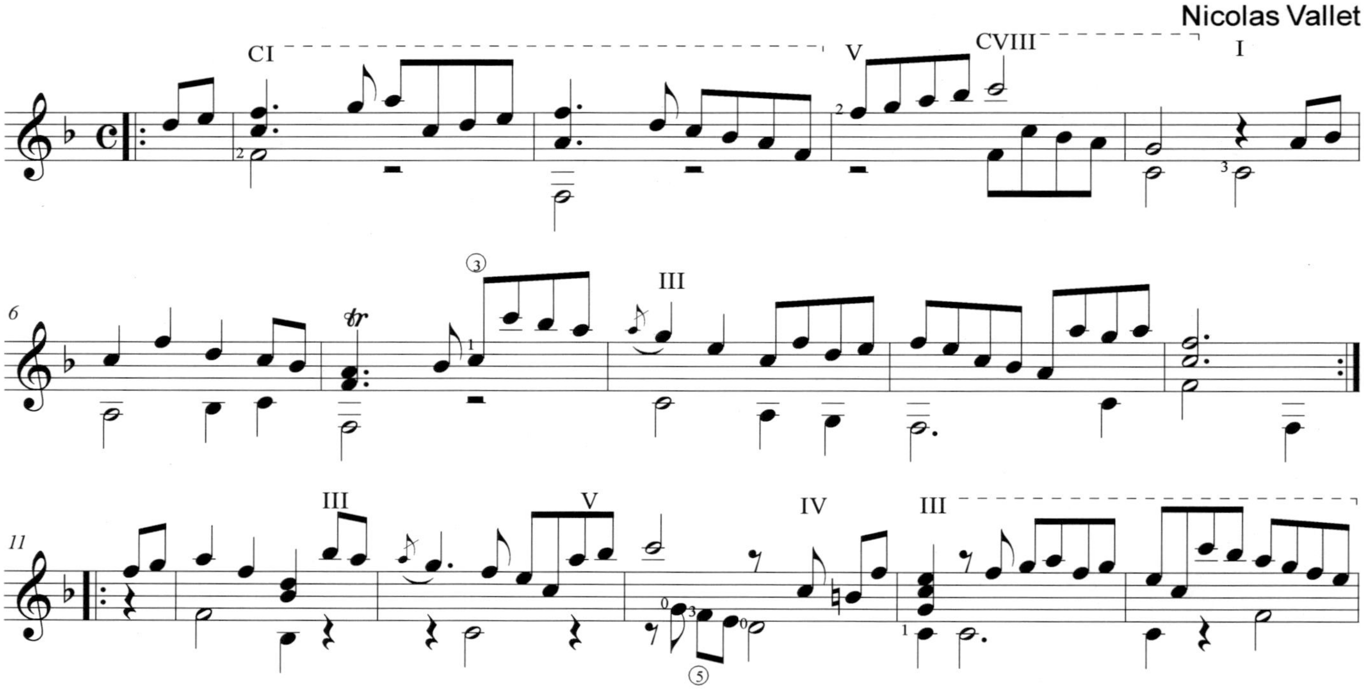

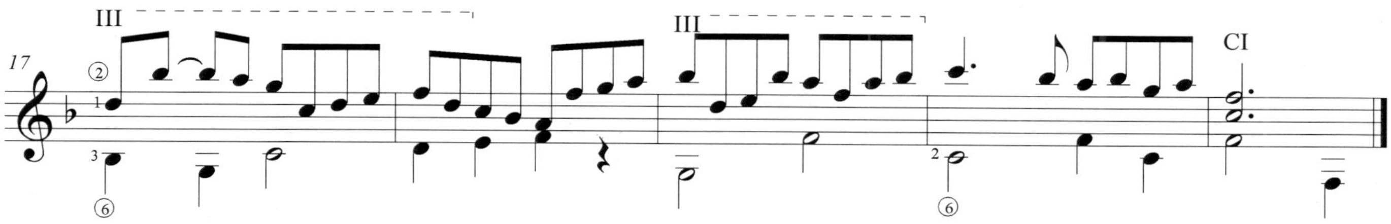

44. La Pincante

Nicolas Vallet

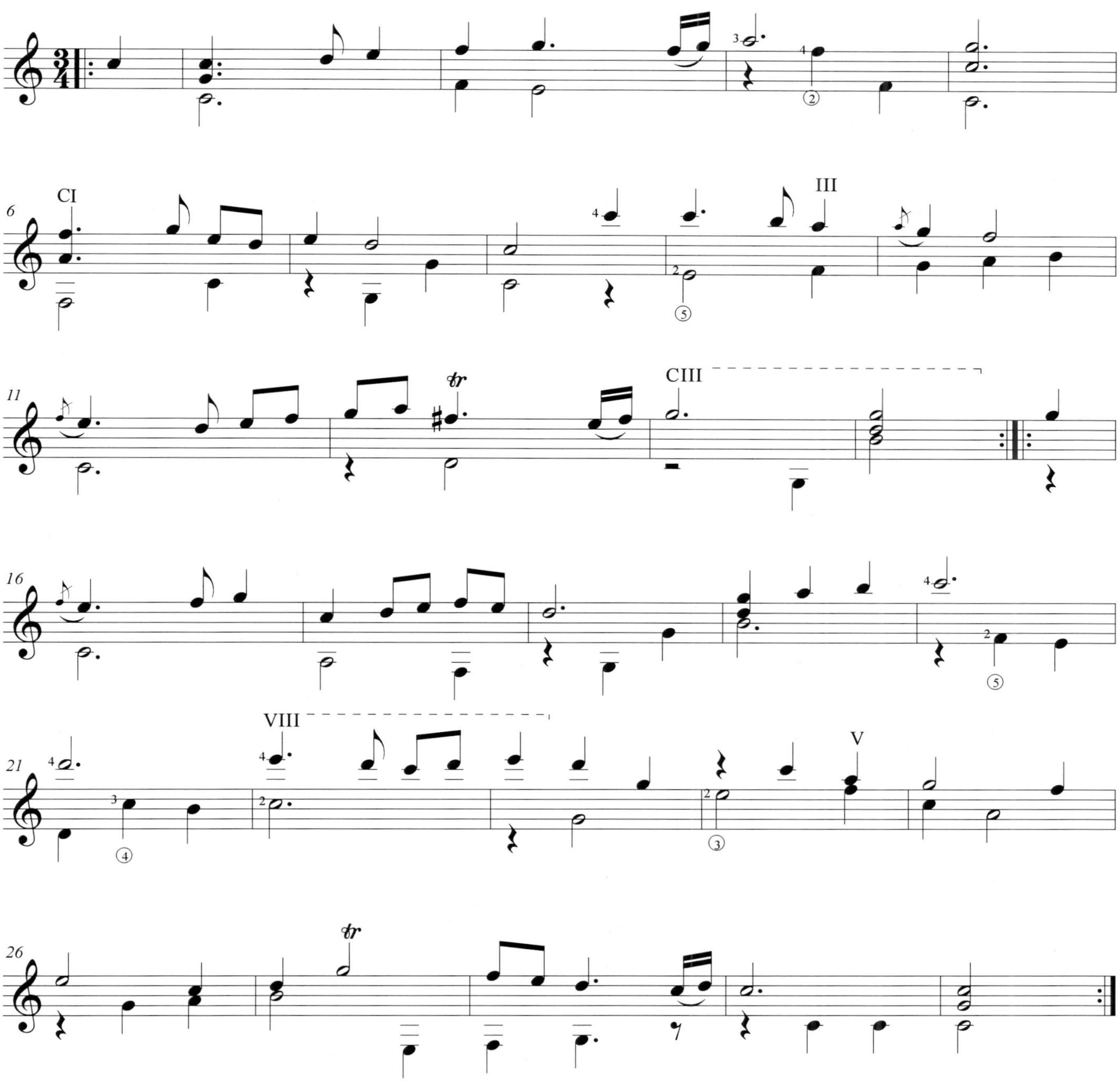

45. La Princesse

Nicolas Vallet

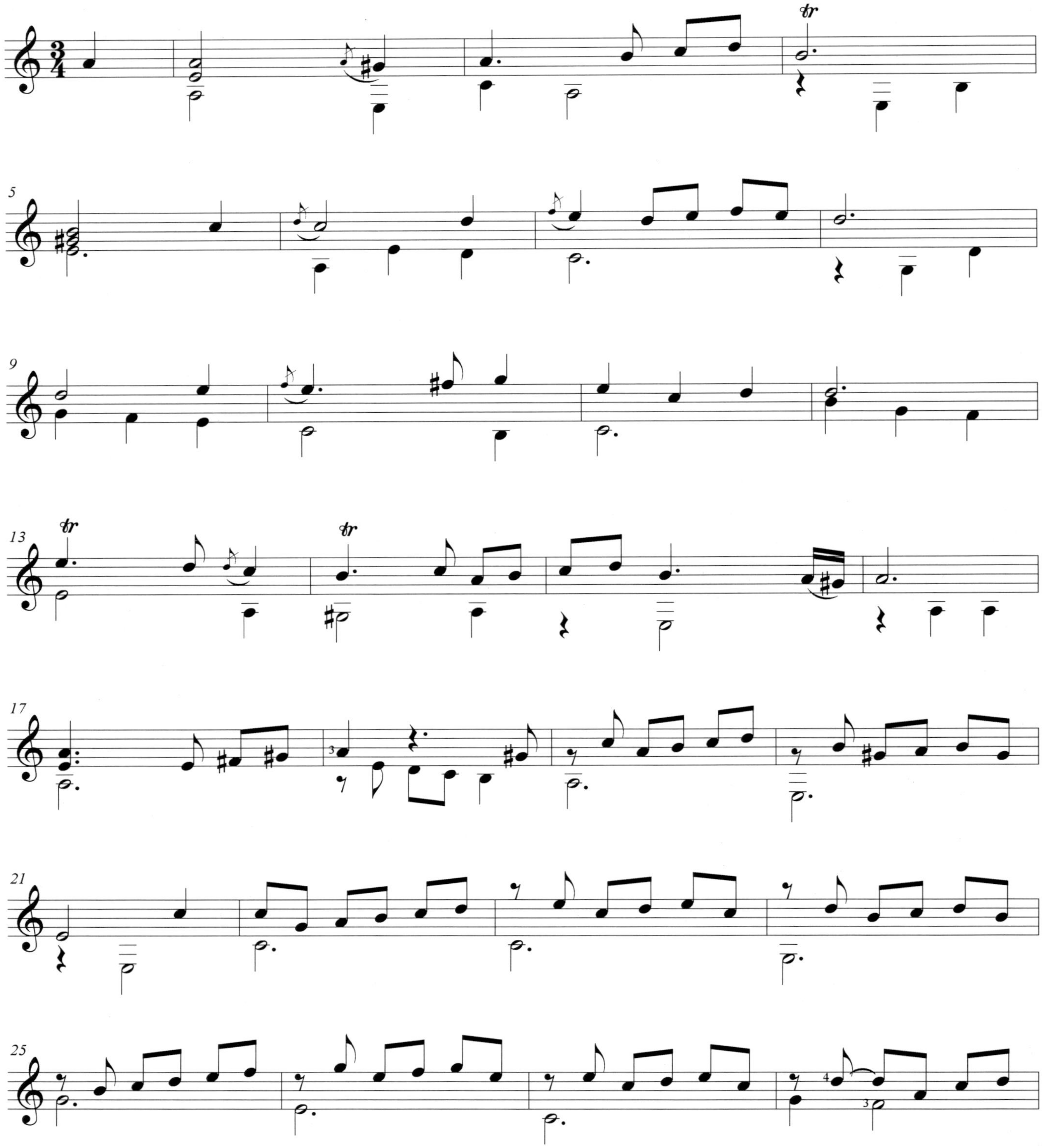

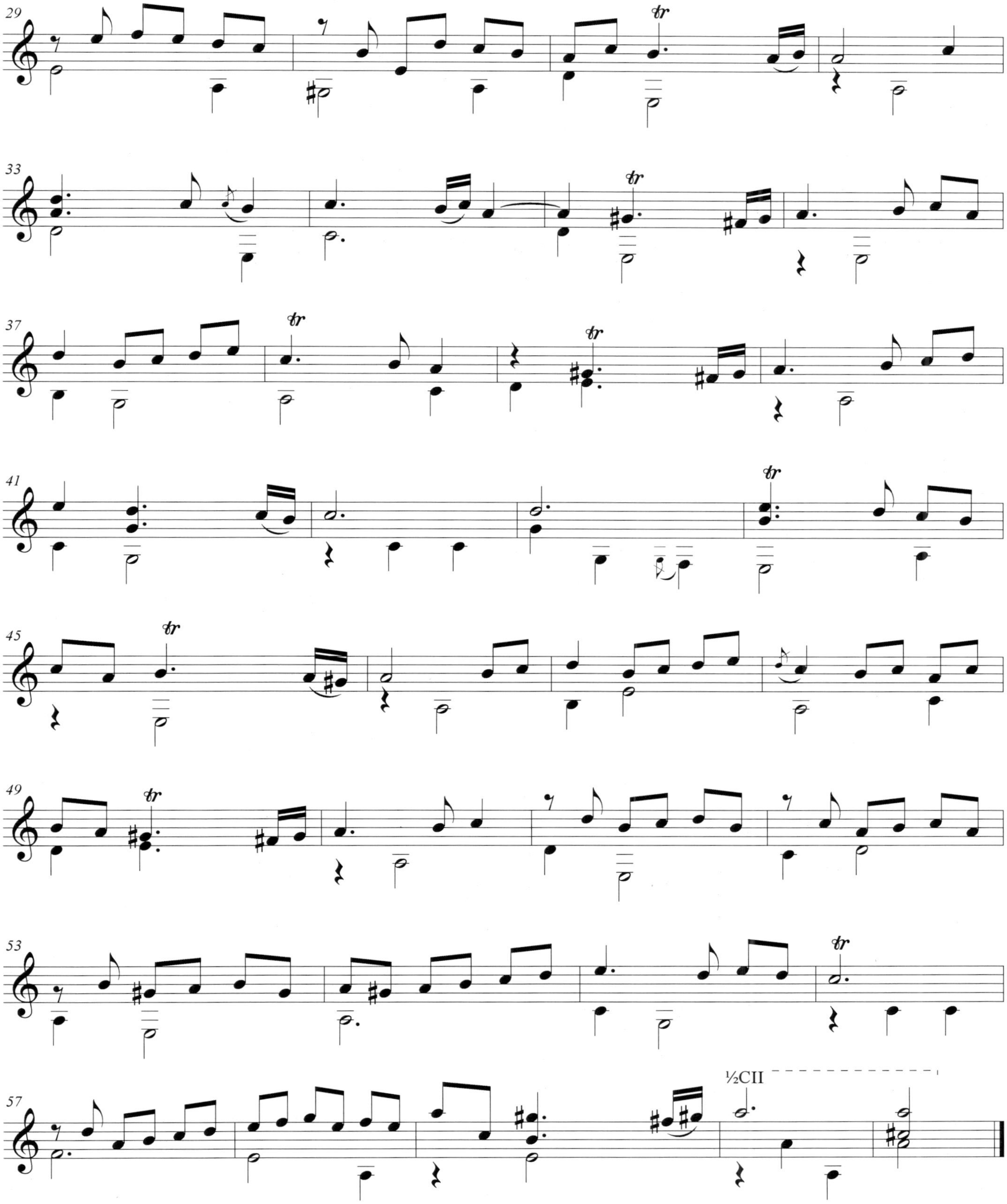
½CII

46. Courante sur la Gaillarde de Bocquet

Nicolas Vallet

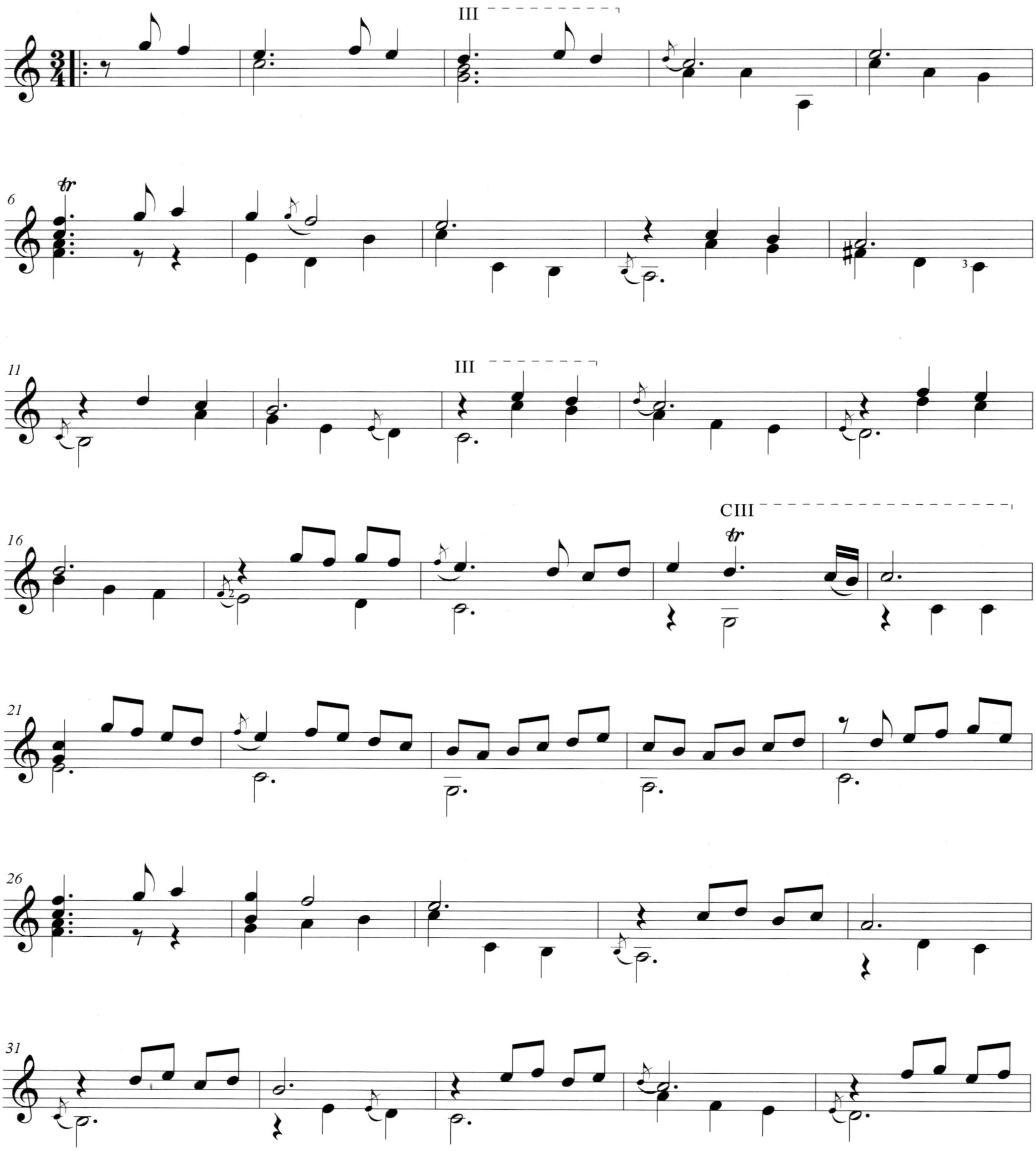

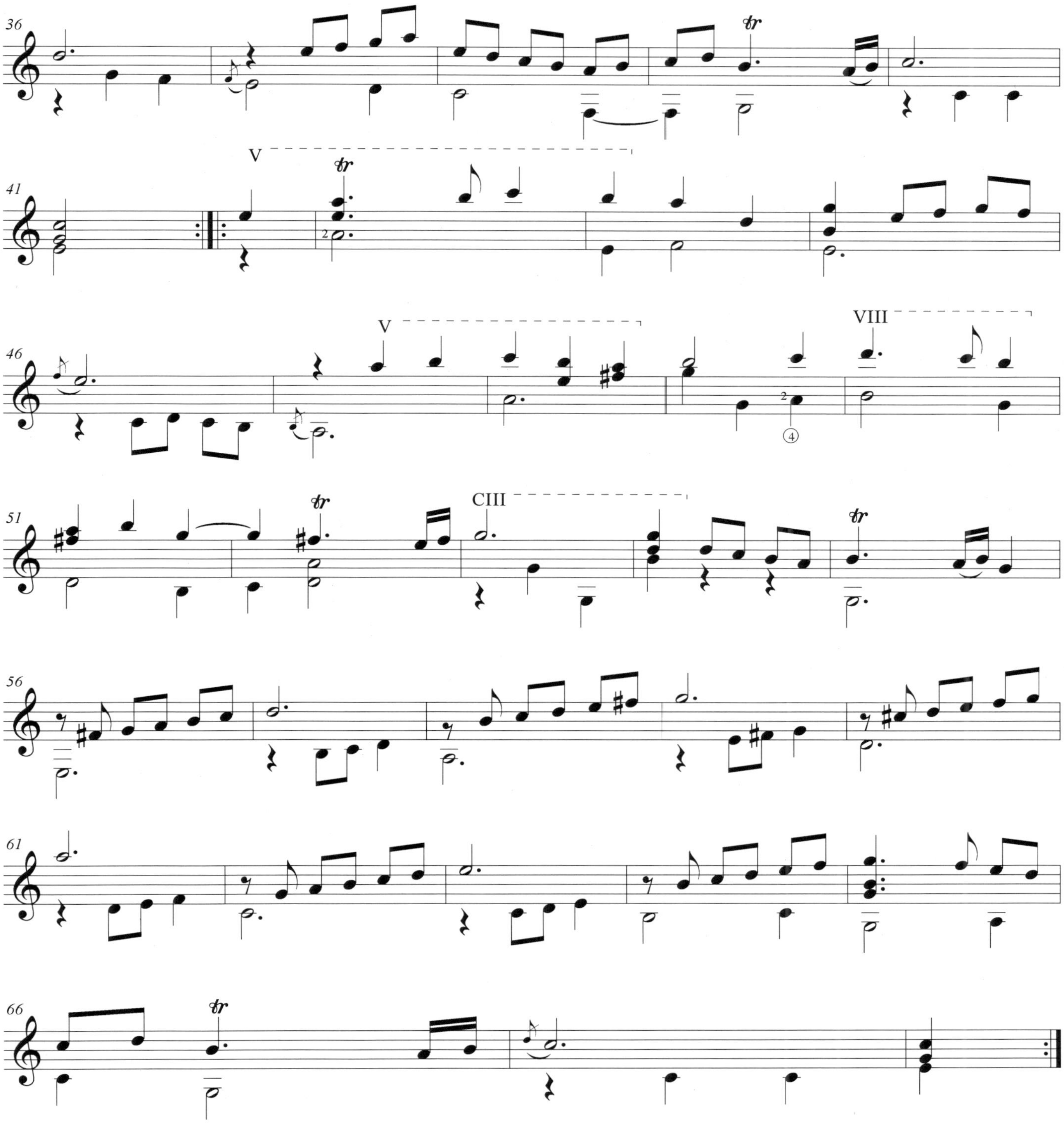
36
41
V
46
V
VIII
51
CIII
56
61
66

47. Aton Bras Droit

Nicolas Vallet

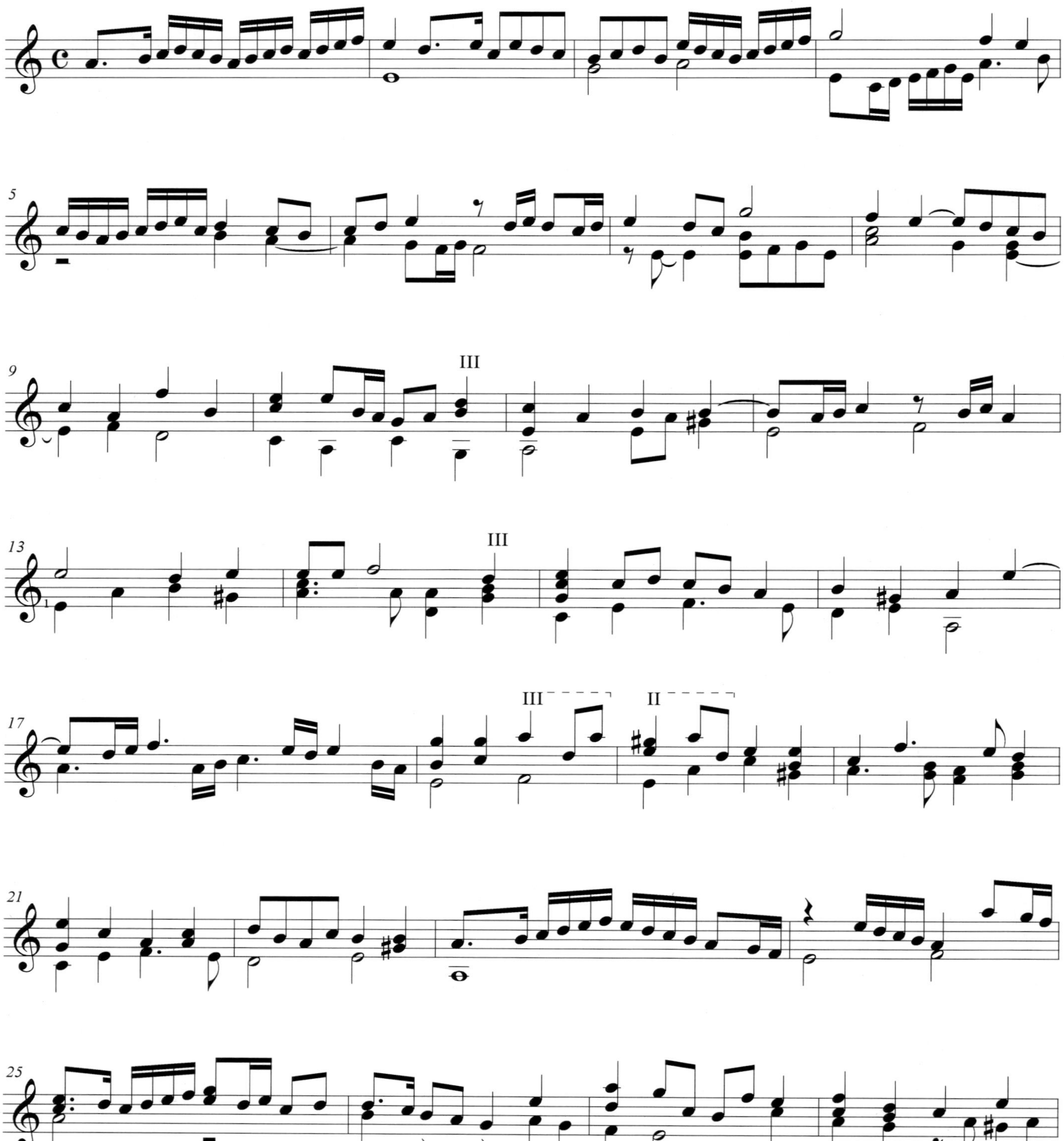

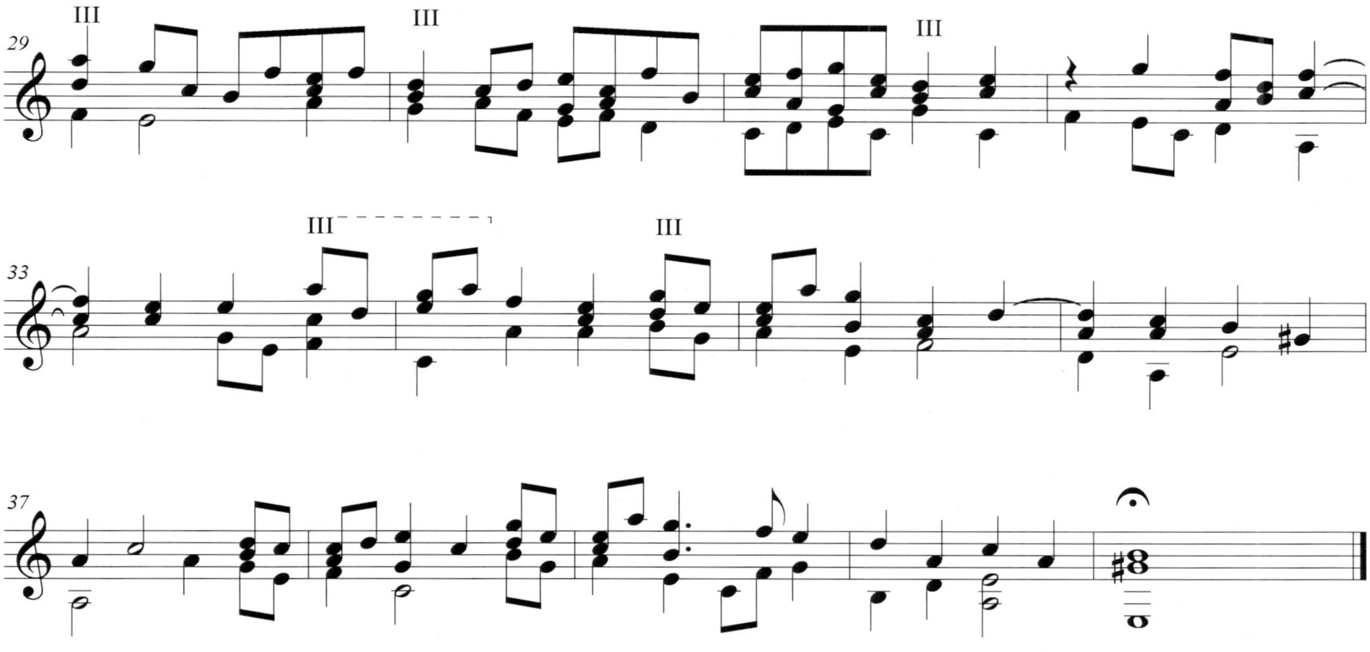
29
III
III
III
33
III
III
37

48. Volte

Nicolas Vallet

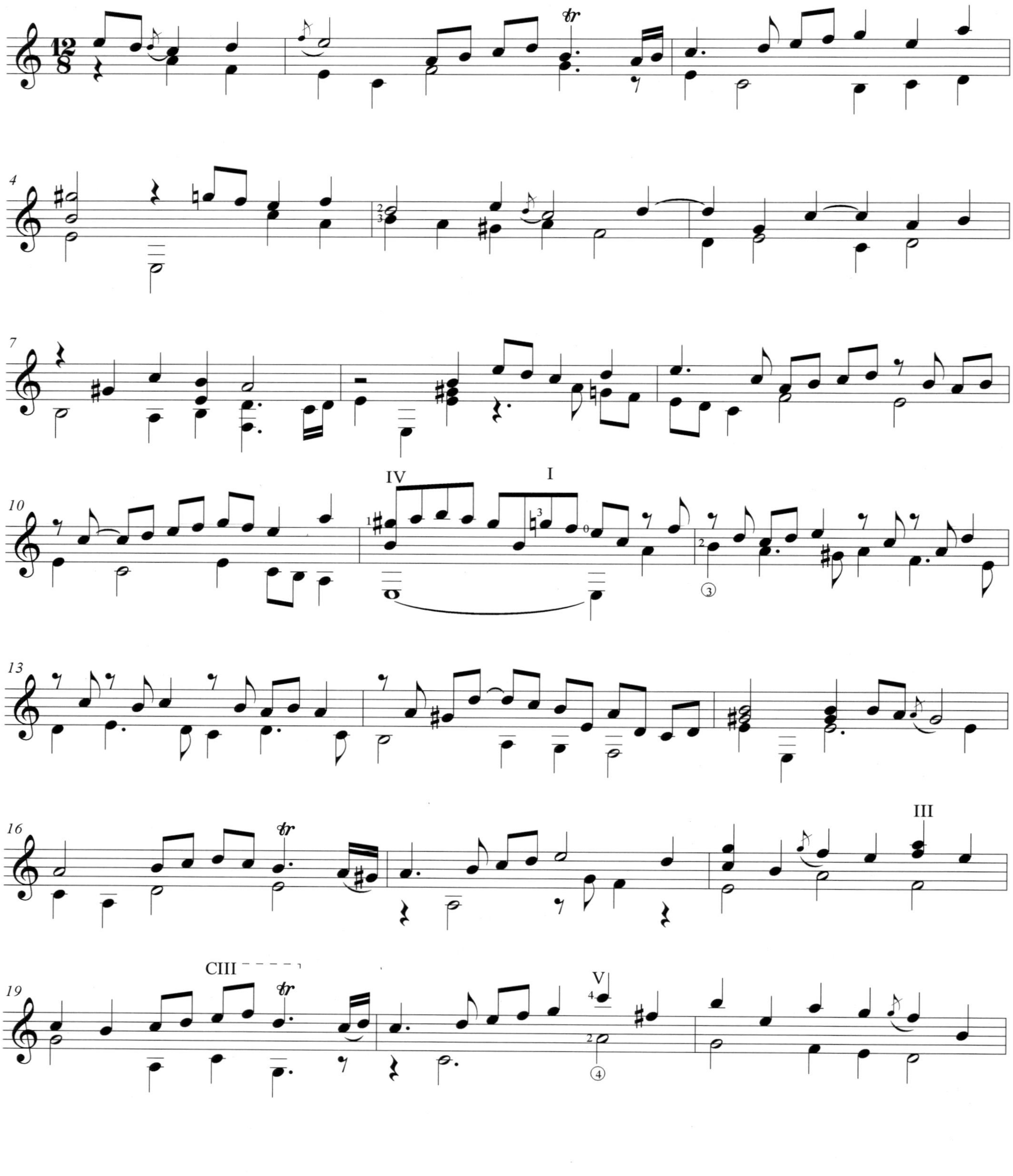

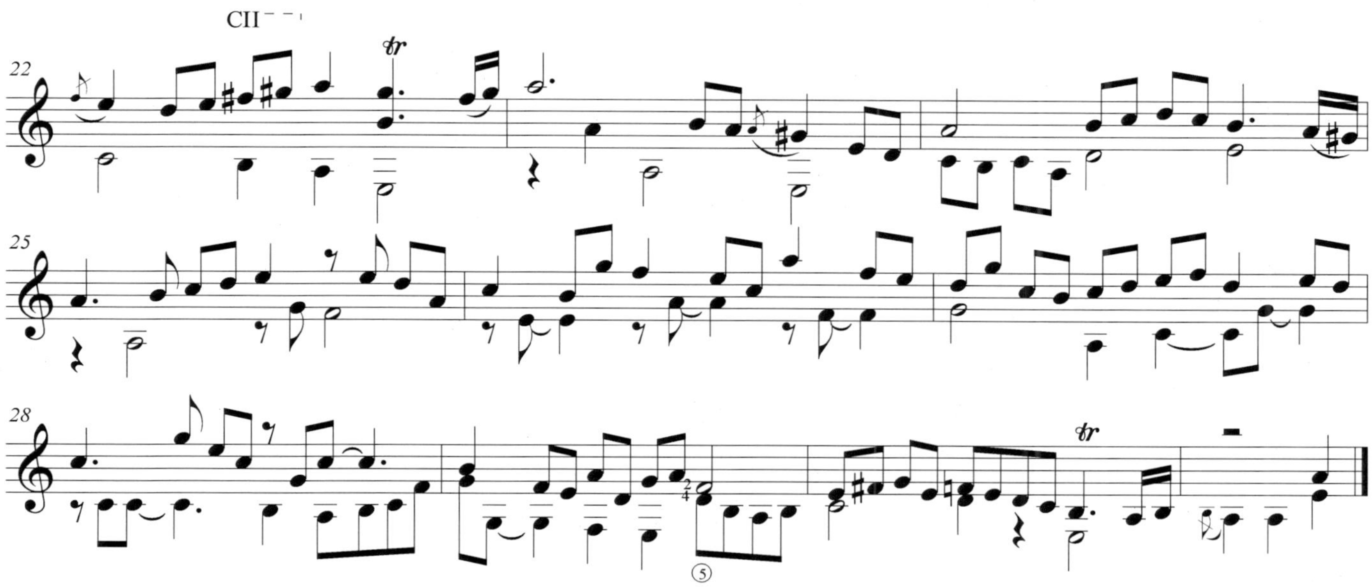
CII
tr
tr
⑤

49. Gaillarde

Nicolas Vallet

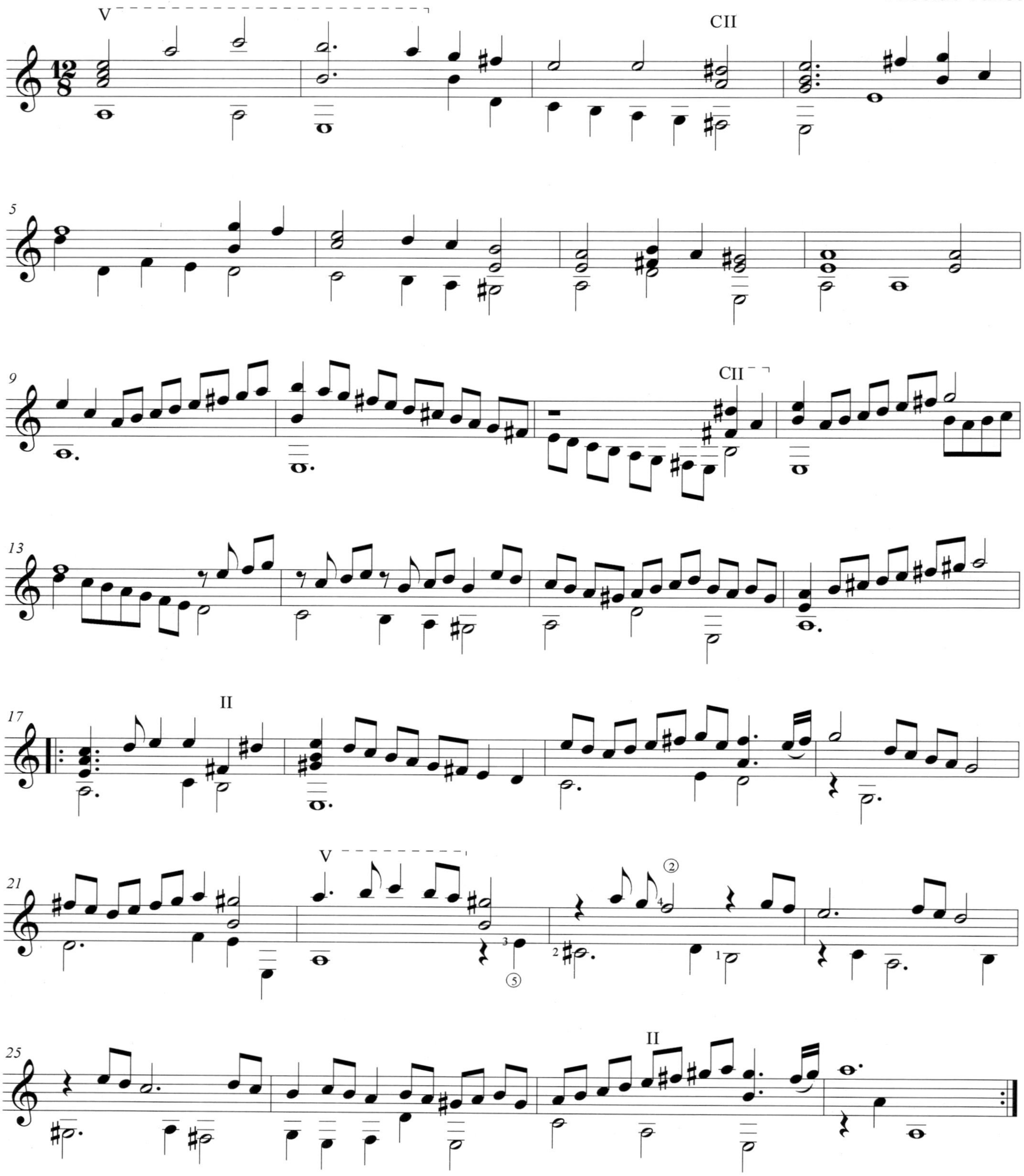

This page has been left blank to avoid an awkward page turn.

50. Passameze d'Italye

Nicolas Vallet

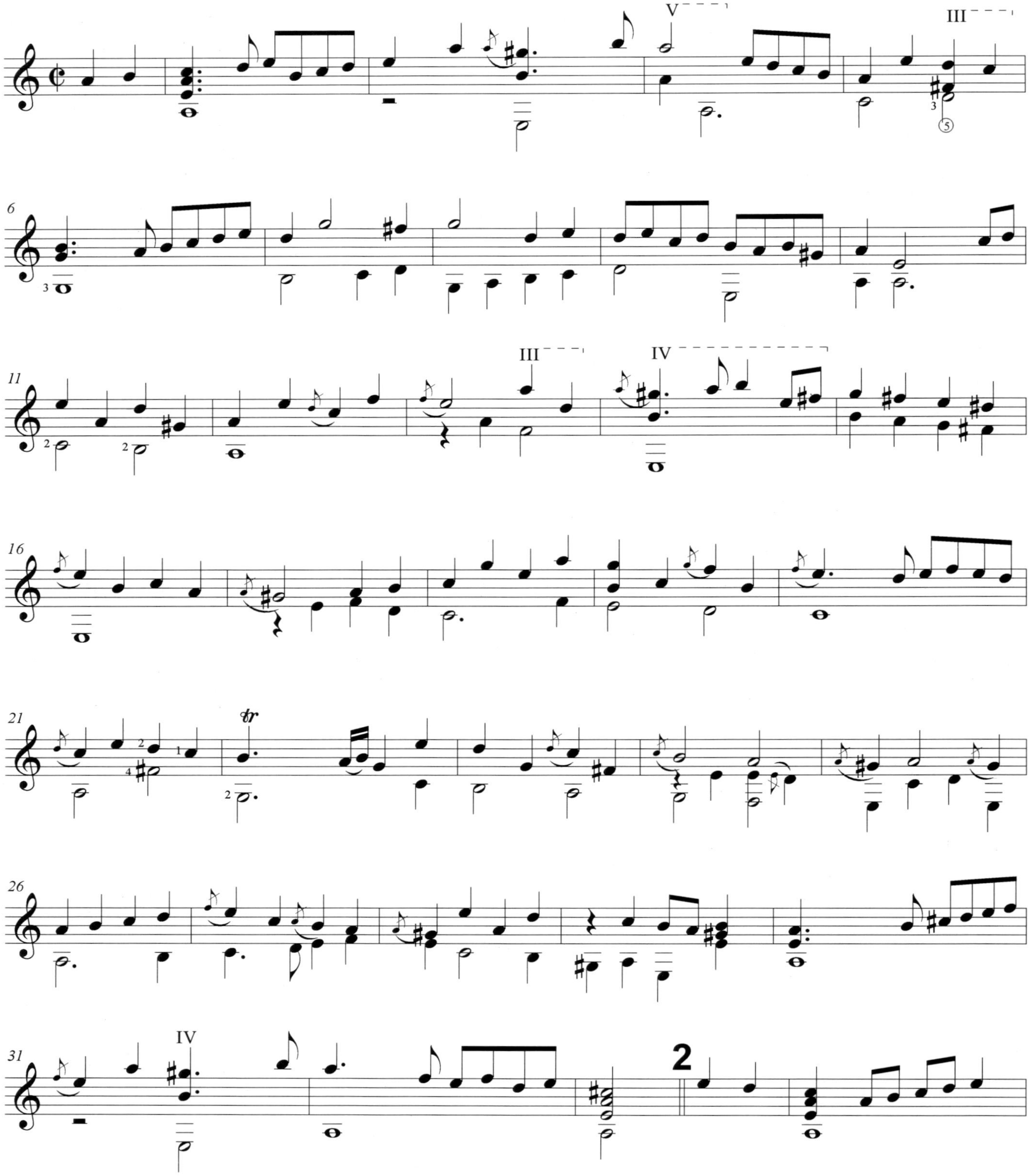

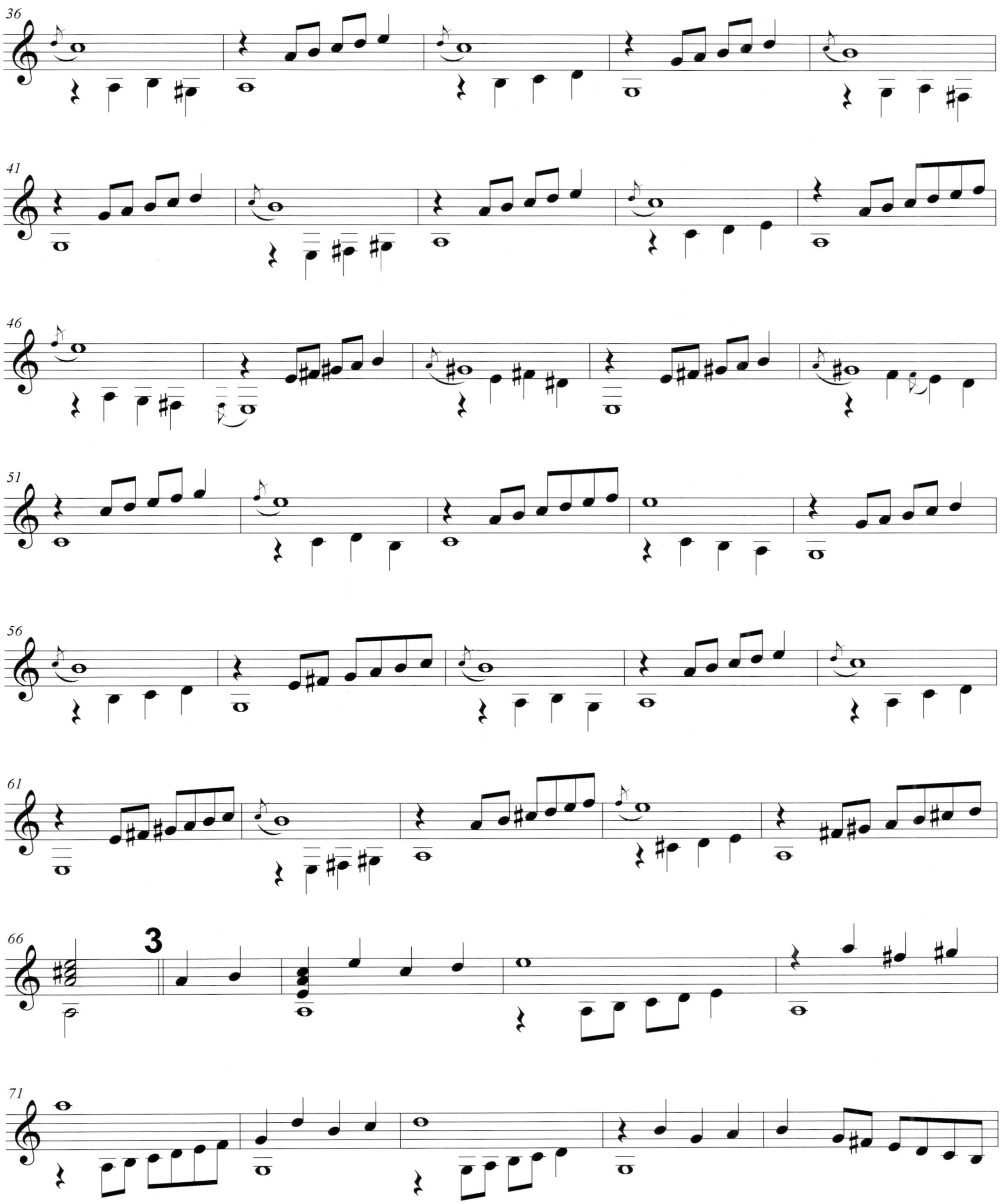
36
41
46
51
56
61
66
3
71

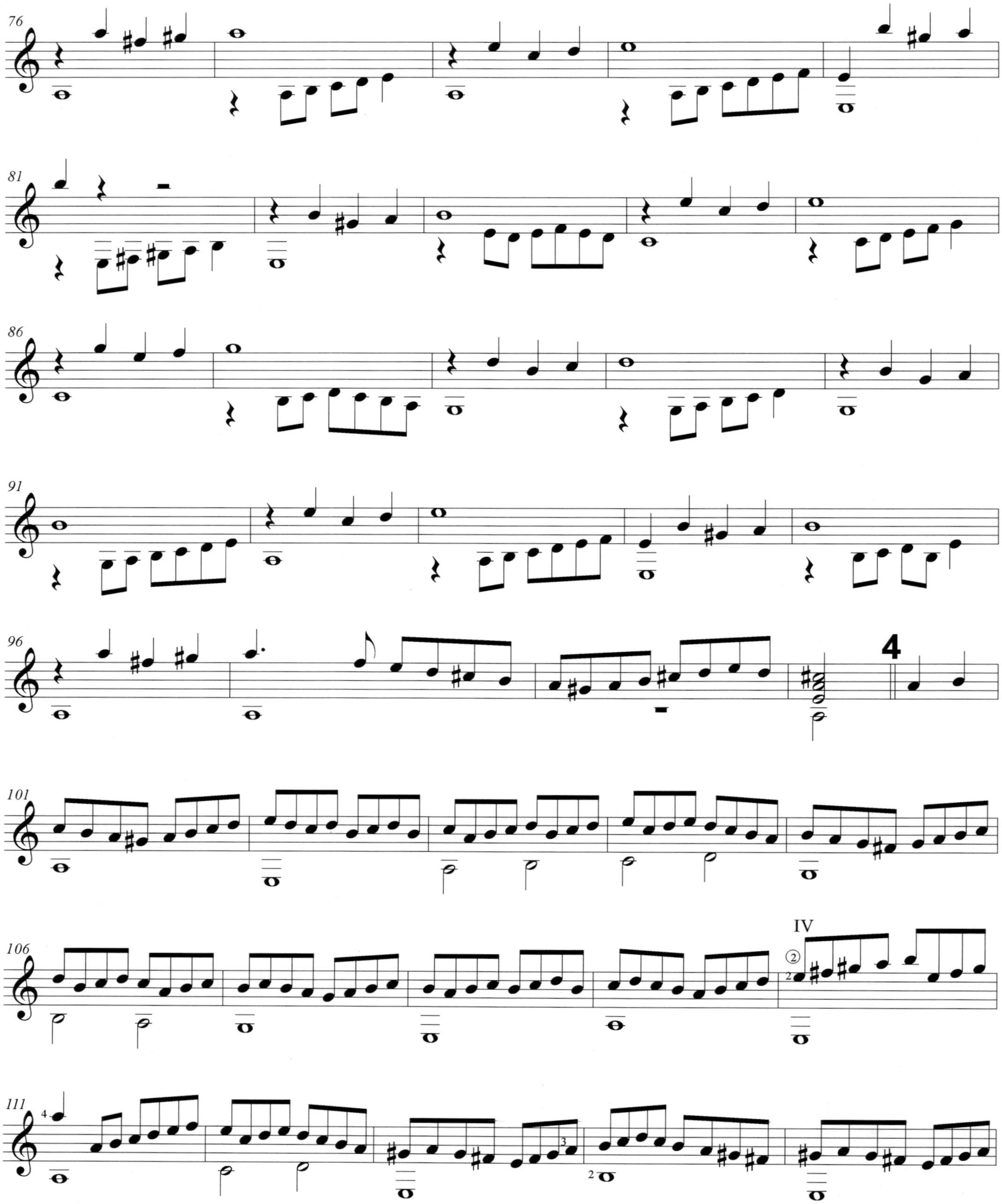
76
81
86
91
96
4
101
106
IV
111

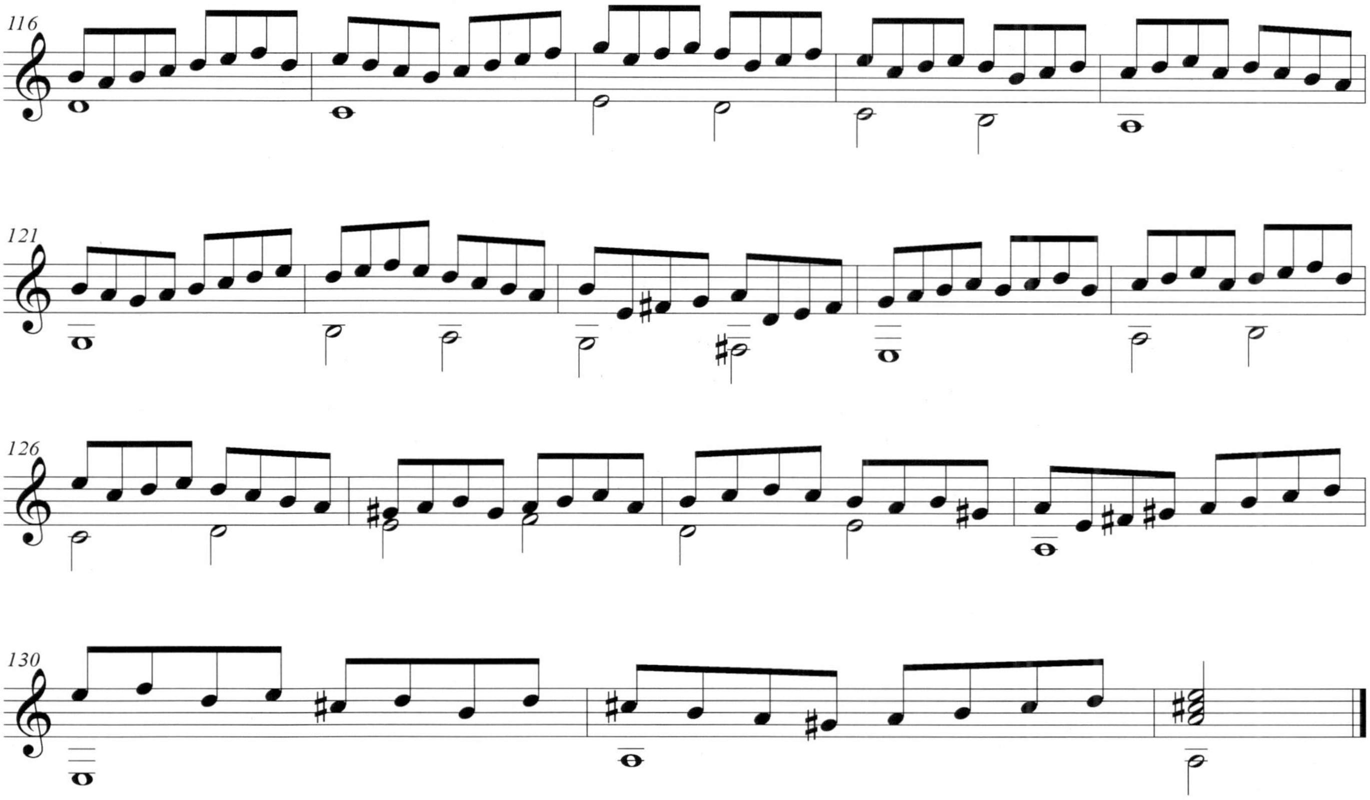
116
121
126
130

51. Gaillarde Angloise

Nicolas Vallet

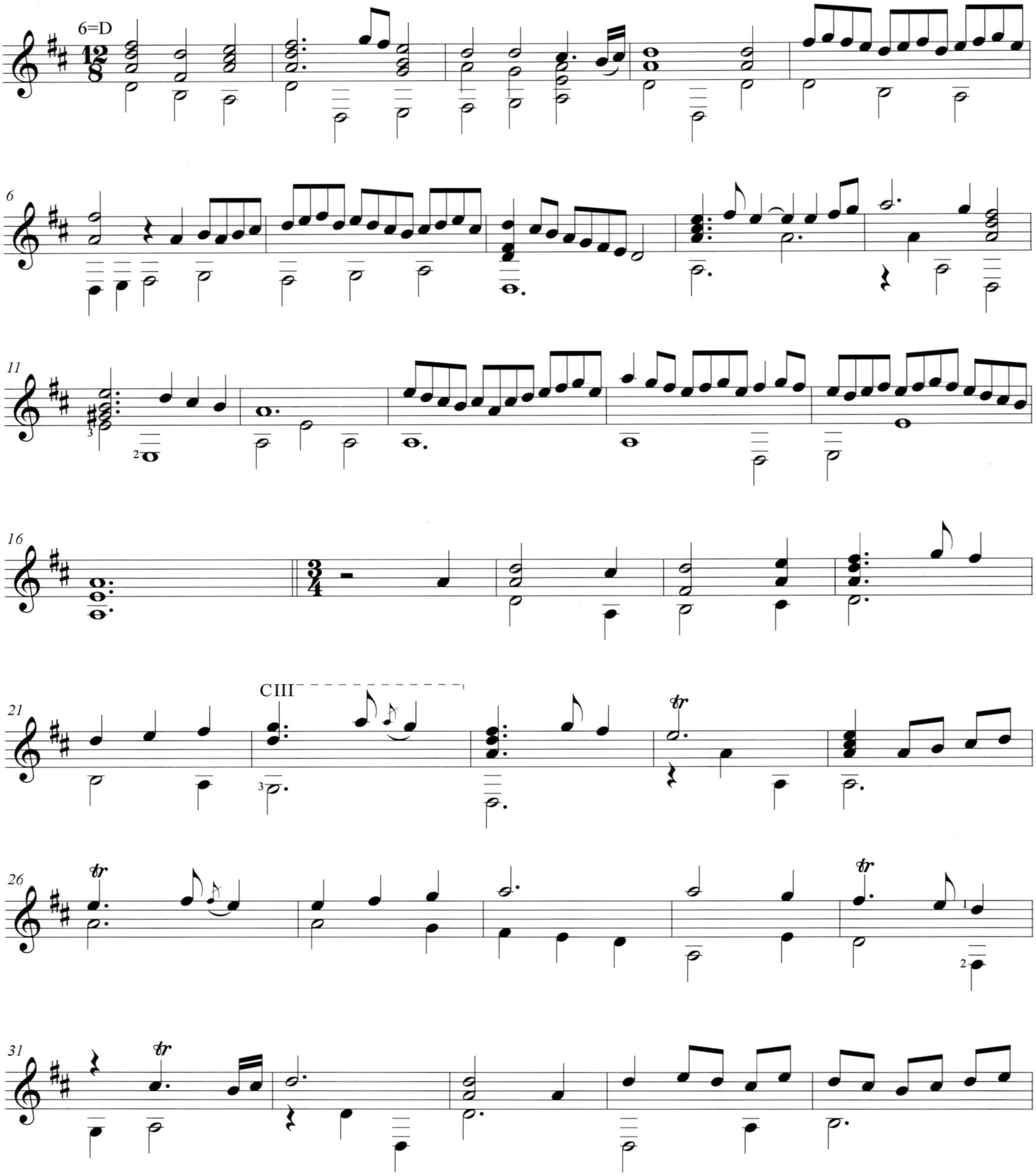

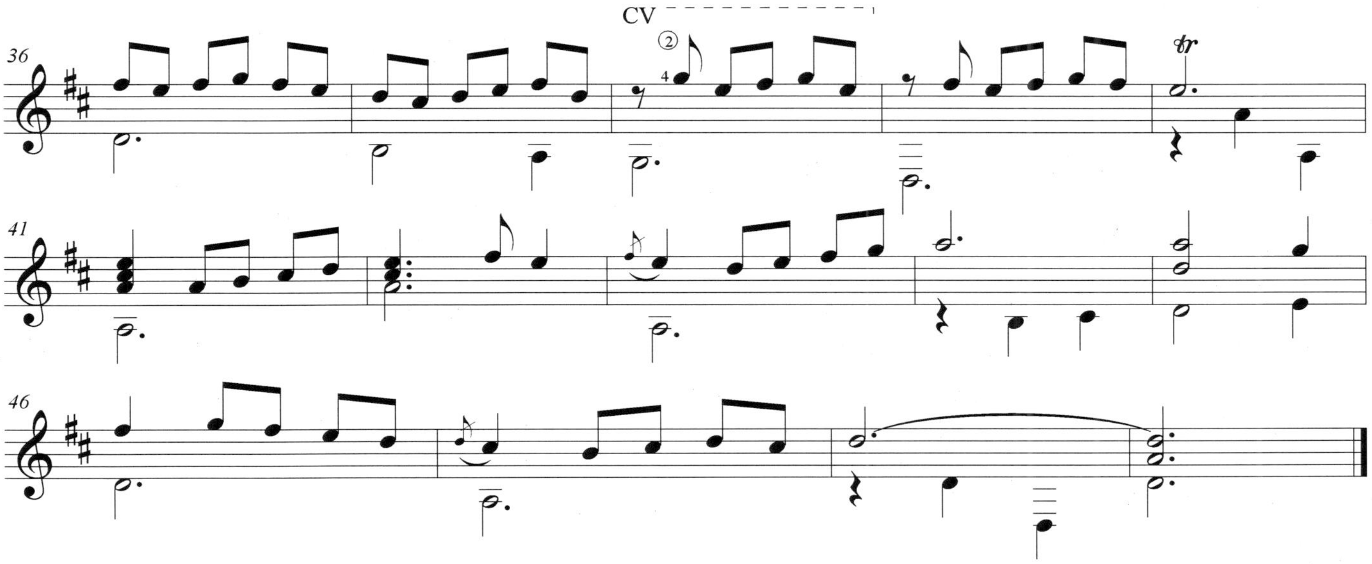
36
CV
tr
41
46

52. Puisque Vosyculs

Nicolas Vallet

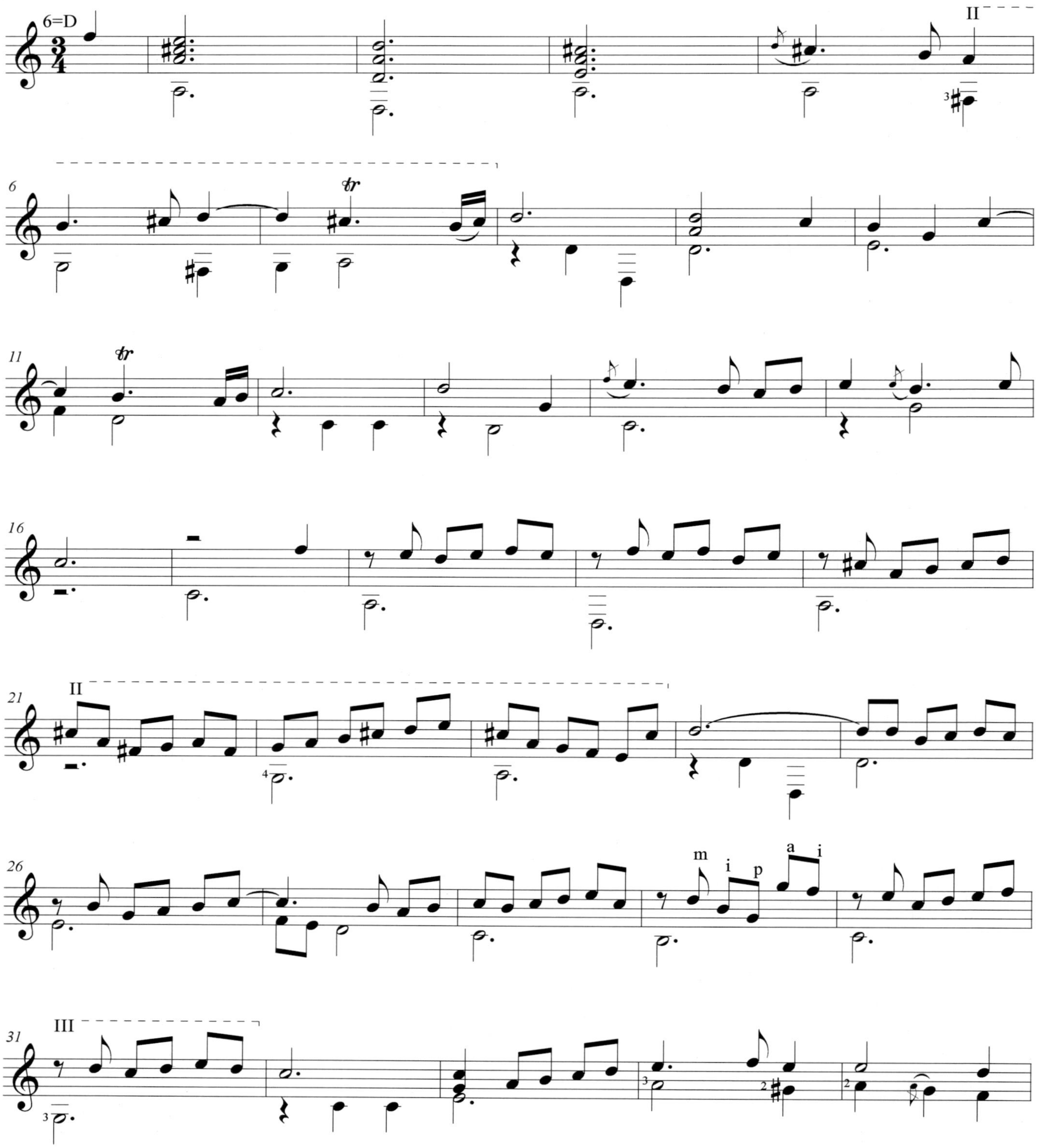

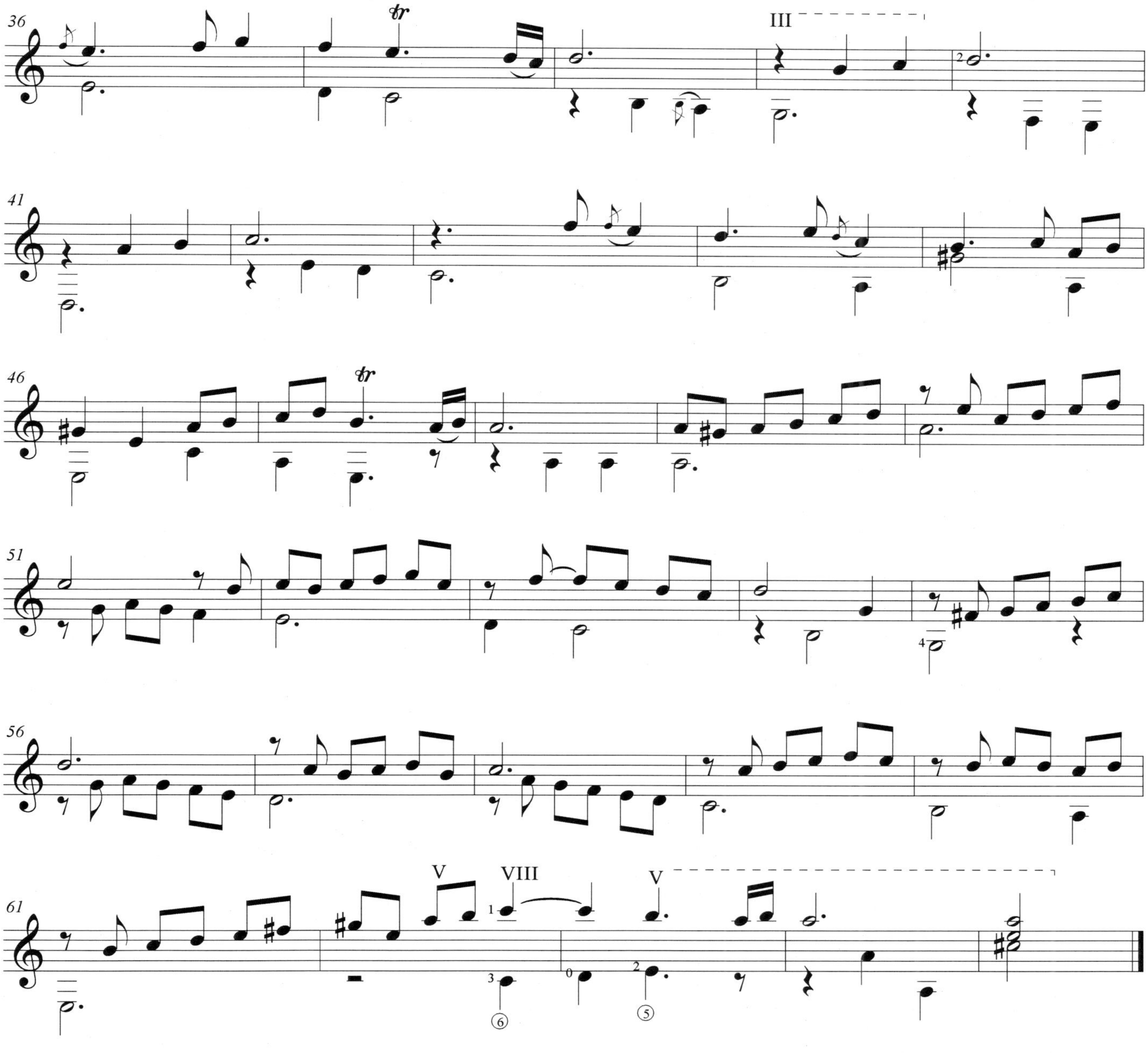
III
V
VIII
V

53. Babdaille

Nicolas Vallet

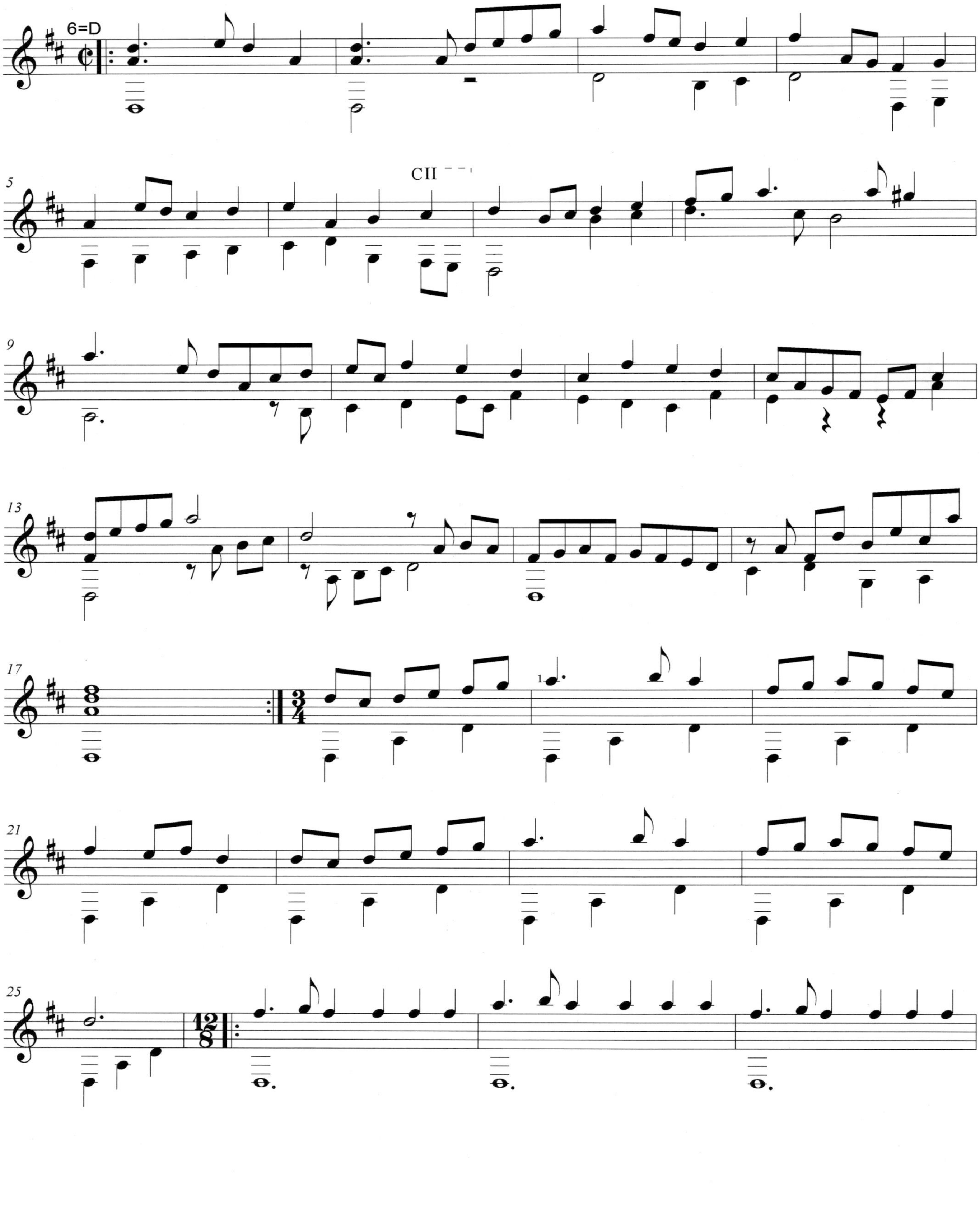

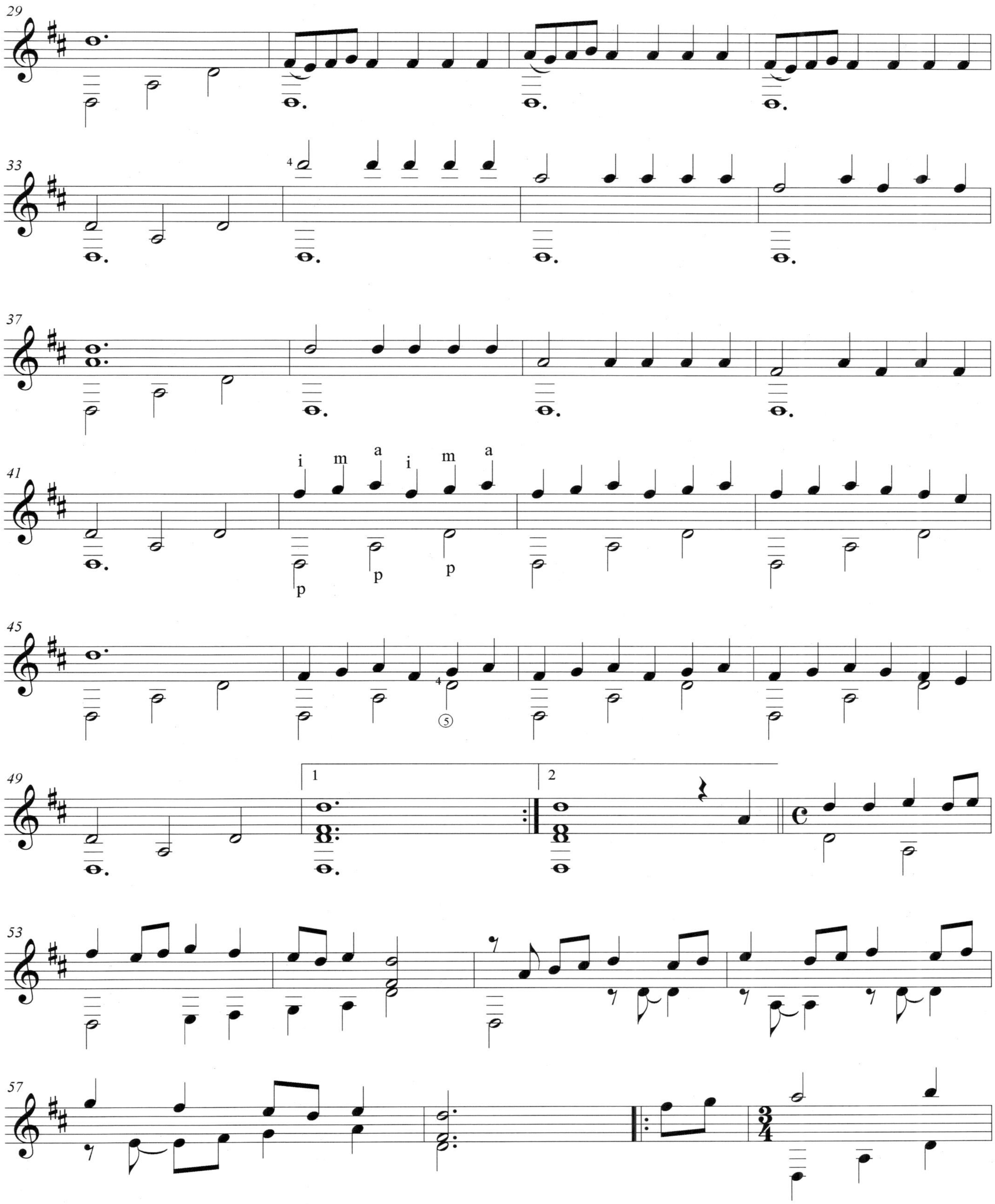
29
33
37
41
i m a i m a
p p p
45
49
1
2
53
57

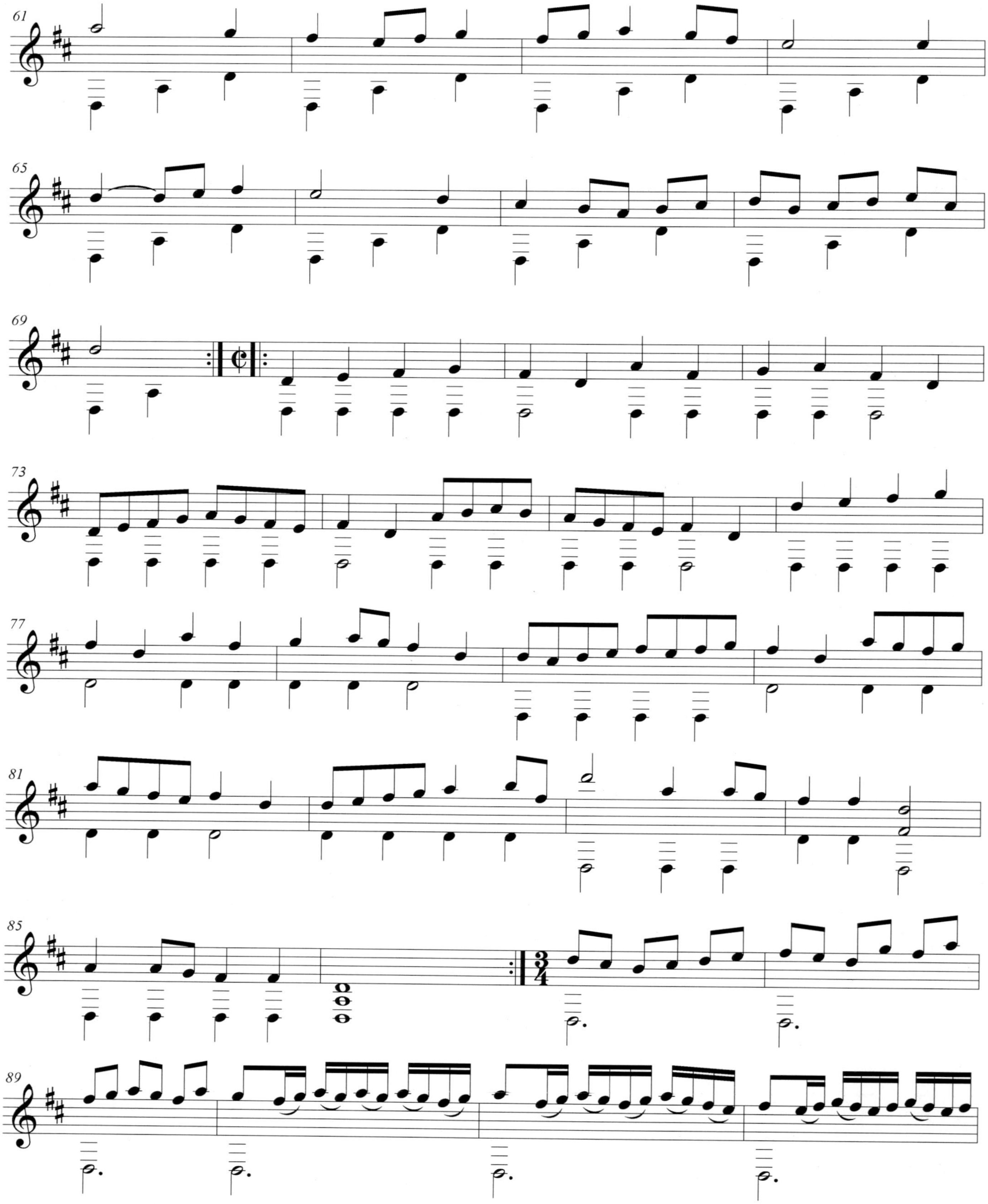
61
65
69
73
77
81
85
89

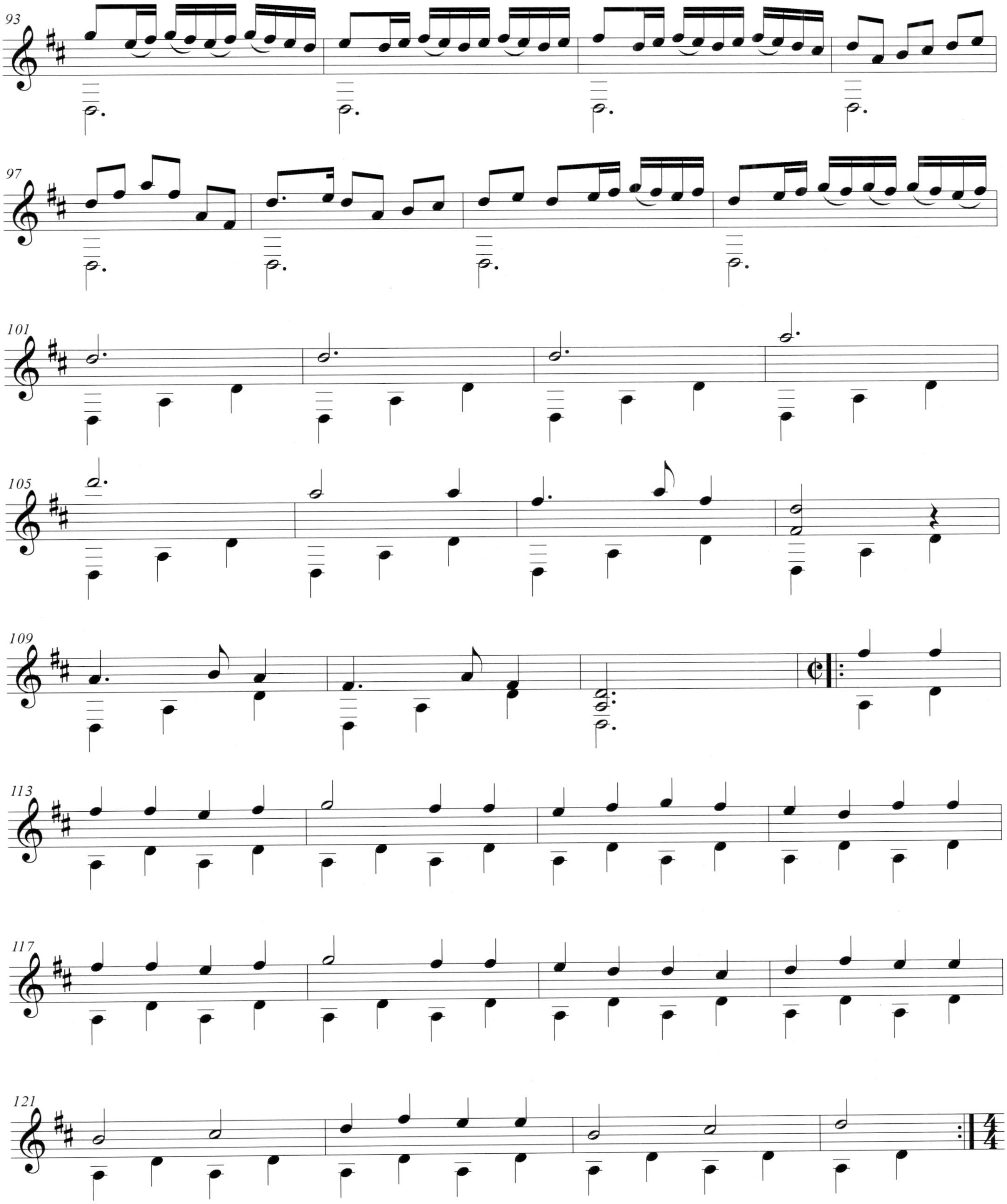
93
97
101
105
109
113
117
121

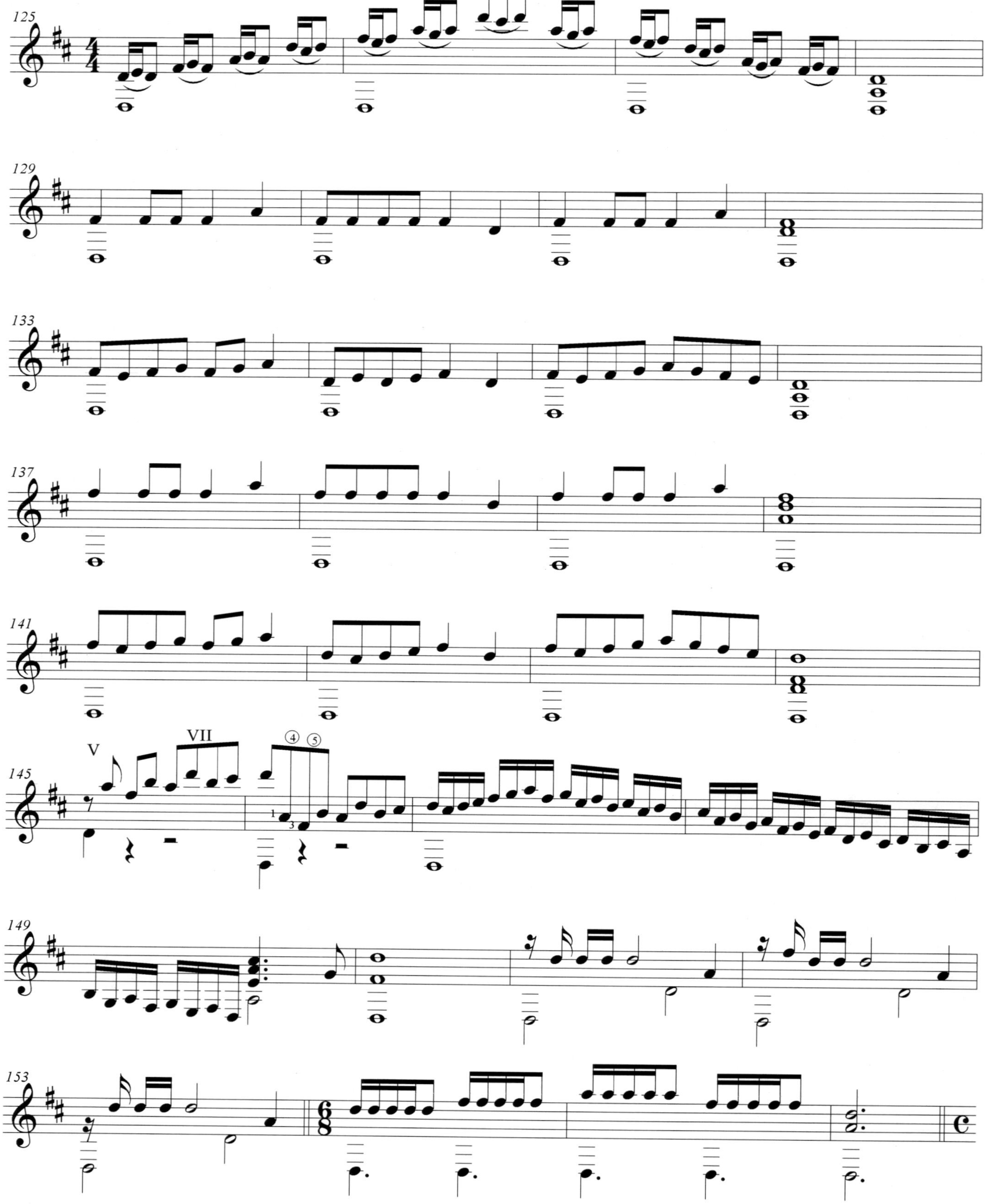
125
129
133
137
141
145
V
VII
④ ⑤
149
153

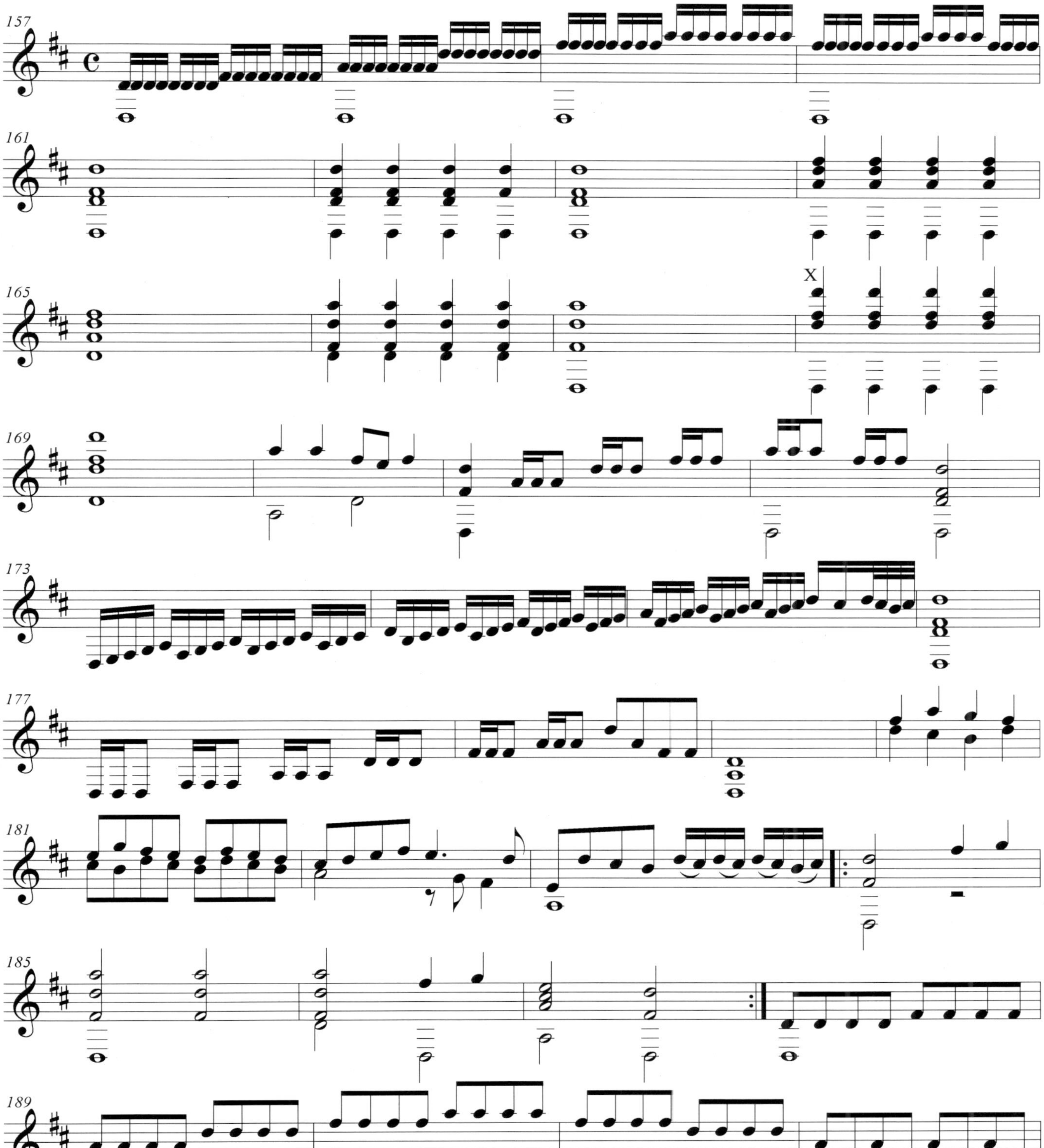
157
161
165
X
169
173
177
181
185
189

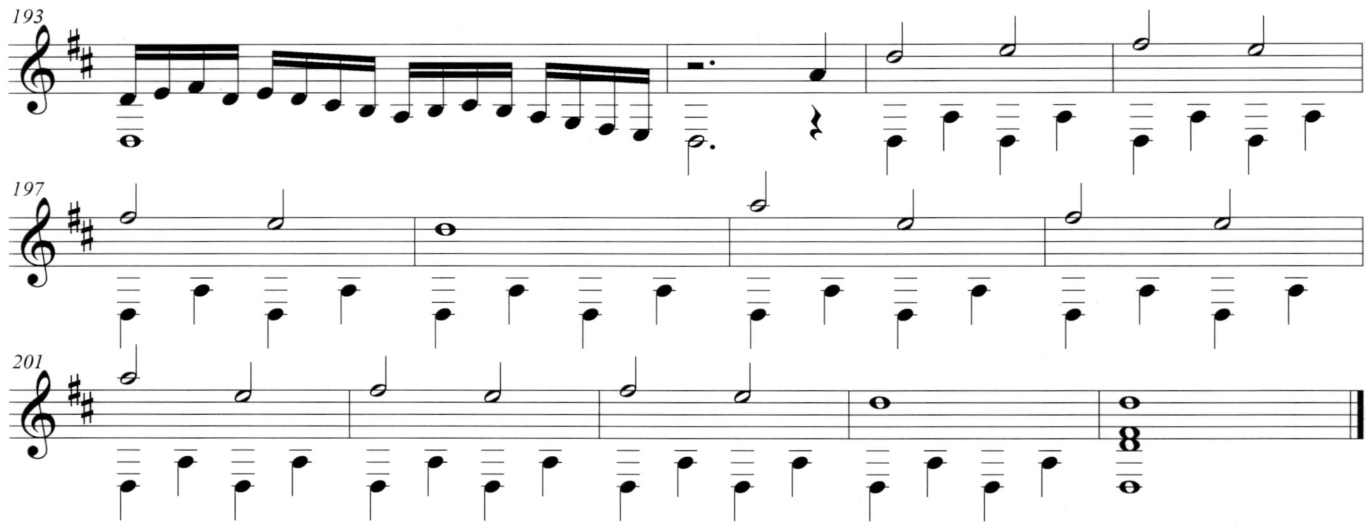
193
197
201

Other Recommended Mel Bay Classic Guitar Solo Collections